MisEducation:
Women and Canadian Universities

MisEducation:
WOMEN &
CANADIAN
UNIVERSITIES

Anne Innis Dagg
Patricia J. Thompson

THE ONTARIO INSTITUTE FOR STUDIES IN EDUCATION

"We can't use non-sexist language; too many people get upset
at the idea of equality."
"We want people to read our journal."

Male students in a mixed group
planning a journal, 1988

The Ontario Institute for Studies in Education has three prime functions: to conduct programs of graduate study in education, to undertake research in education, and to assist in the implementation of the findings of educational studies. The Institute is a college chartered by an Act of the Ontario Legislature in 1965. It is affiliated with the University of Toronto for graduate studies purposes.

The publications program of the Institute has been established to make available information and materials arising from studies in education, to foster the spirit of critical inquiry, and to provide a forum for the exchange of ideas about education. The opinions expressed should be viewed as those of the contributors.

Canadian Cataloguing in Publication Data
Dagg, Anne Innis, 1933-
  MisEducation : women and Canadian universities
(Monograph ; 18)
Bibliography: p.
ISBN 0-7744-0318-7

1. Sex discrimination in education — Canada.
2. Women — Education — Canada. 3. Women in education
— Canada. 4. Universities and colleges — Canada.
I. Thompson, Patricia J., 1967- . II. Ontario Institute
for Studies in Education. III. Title. IV. Series:
Monograph series (Ontario Institute for Studies in
Education) ; 18.

LC1766.D33 1988   370.19'345   C88-093660-6

ISBN 0-7744-0318-7   Printed in Canada
1 2 3 4 5 WEBCOM 29 19 09 98 88

Contents

Preface

In 1987, while writing this book, we visited a number of universities and related institutions to see what they offered women in the way of women's studies courses, women's centres, recreation, and childcare. They were: Carleton University, Ontario Institute for Studies in Education, Oxford University, U.K., Ryerson Institute of Technology, Simon Fraser University, Trent University, University of British Columbia, University of Calgary, University of Guelph, University of Ottawa, University of Toronto, University of Waterloo, Wilfrid Laurier University, and York University.

In recent years we have also visited Dalhousie University, McGill University, McMaster University, St. Francis Xavier University, St. Mary's University, University of Manitoba, University of New Brunswick, University of Prince Edward Island, University of Saskatchewan, University of Victoria, and the University of Western Ontario.

This is not a book of history, detailing the ups and downs of women and academia over the years. That tale has been well told by Gisele Marie Thibault in *The Dissenting Feminist Academy: A History of the Barriers to Feminist Scholarship* (1987). Rather, it is an account of what is actually going on at Canadian universities today, a reality which is not an attractive one. We have gathered information from a wide variety of sources, all of them recent, and all representative, we feel, of what is happening across Canada. If we deal with some topics less thoroughly than others, it is because the data available are sometimes limited. We hope that this book will engender discussion in such areas and about all aspects of the present uneasy relationship between women and universities.

We would like to thank the many women who provided us with information about their universities for this book. We shall not name them here, so that no reprisal can be taken against them. We owe much to our editor, Frances Rooney, who has been both indefatigable and enthusiastic in the refining of our manuscript for publication. We are also most grateful to Jean Spowart who typed many drafts of the text.

We dedicate this book to the unbiased universities that Canada could have in the future, and to the university women of Canada willing to work toward this goal.

Anne Innis Dagg
Patricia J. Thompson

January, 1988

Introduction

What we have at present is a man-centered university, a breeding ground not of humanism, but of masculine privilege. As women have gradually and reluctantly been admitted into the mainstream of higher education, they have been made participants in a system that prepares men to take up roles of power in a man-centered society, that asks questions and teaches "facts" generated by a male intellectual tradition, and that both subtly and openly confirms men as the leaders and shapers of human destiny both within and outside academia. The exceptional women who have emerged from this system and who hold distinguished positions in it are just that: the required exceptions used by every system to justify and maintain itself.

Adrienne Rich
On Lies, Secrets, and Silence, 1979

'What we [feminists] are doing is comparable to Copernicus shattering our geo-centricity, Darwin shattering our species-centricity. We are shattering andro-centricity, and the change is as fundamental, as dangerous, as exciting.' And we are surprised that we are not welcome in the academy?

Elizabeth Minnich
quoted in Bowles and Klein
Theories of Women's Studies, 1983

This book has three aims. One is to point out the extent of sexual discrimination and bias that occurs in Canadian universities. The second is to expose the incredible anti-woman ambience that presently exists in academia and that undermines the confidence and self-respect of all women scholars. The third is to offer recommendations that, if implemented, would greatly ameliorate the situation of university women. We hope that people reading this book will pressure administrators and professors to eradicate sexism in higher education. We hope that in the future universities will be places that foster, rather than inhibit or at best grudgingly tolerate, the development of women's full intellectual potential.

1

What Happens in Universities Matters

If universities were truly the ivory towers that some people maintain they are, then it would not matter so much that professors overwhelmingly disseminate information pertinent to men, from men's perspective, and largely about men; that women and men students must still learn this information as "truth" if they wish to graduate; and that research focusses on problems of interest to men. This busy making and sharing of "knowledge" would be done in a vacuum, without affecting the rest of society.

But universities are *not* ivory towers. The students they indoctrinate with male-biased knowledge go out into the world carrying with them what they have learned. As doctors, lawyers, professors, and other professionals they are in powerful positions to disseminate their male-centred ideas through the entire social fabric. And everyone who has contact with a university learns that men are more important than women, and that men's ideas are the ones that matter.

When our society looks at its universities, it sees not the leaders it might expect, but rigidly hierarchical institutions immersed in conservative values. It sees elitist establishments not much interested in exploring new avenues and alternatives in life, but fiercely defending the status quo. It sees few women professors, for all Canadian universities practise sexual discrimination, and no will to carry out extensive research related to long-ignored women's issues. Worst of all, it sees places where its daughters are short changed, where young women are funnelled into disciplines that lead to low-paying jobs, and are taught that women are less important than men.

Universities cost Canadian taxpayers over $5 billion a year (*Canada Yearbook,* 1988, pp. 4–5). Women have a right to expect that this money should help, rather than hinder as it now does, their progress toward equality in society with men.

Why We Wrote This Book

When I entered university two years ago, I expected to encounter teachers and researchers searching honestly to contribute to their areas of inquiry. I expected that all students would be encouraged to work hard in order to develop their talents into proficiencies. Instead, I have increasingly found that selection processes are being used to screen both information and human resources. The selection process discussed in this book is based not on an objective measure of merit, but on the unjust and indefensible ideology of sexism.

I have found that although women have been attending universities for over a century, our presence there remains an anomaly in the minds of many powerful people in the university hierarchy. As a result, the expansion of the abilities of most talented women is curtailed long before it reaches its natural limits. This wasting of potential occurs at all levels of the university system: a female undergraduate is discouraged by her professors from studying a male-dominated discipline such as engineering; a graduate student's research about women is not funded; a young female professor is denied tenure. This unfair discrimination is often carried out in insidious fashion, at the same time that administrators pledge their commitment to raising the status of women in the university community. This element of deception renders the insult to women even more reprehensible.

Beyond the visible results of sex discrimination, I have found a more pernicious process. Instead of creating a climate that favors increased equality, sexist practices in the university contribute to the perception among female and male students, faculty, and staff that women's lower status is part of the natural order. The language and course materials used in teaching are tainted by the same stereotypes that thwart the full development of people of both sexes in society. Women are subjected to an environment of sexism, sexual harassment, and sexual assault that interferes with their full participation in, and enjoyment of, the experience of university, yet we are led to believe that this is a normal part of life. Feminists, whose goal is to correct the inequalities between women and men for the greater benefit of all, are incessantly censored and scorned for their attempts to present a woman's point of view. Living in this atmosphere, witnessing the suffering of the women around me, and hearing the almost unvarying institutional response of silence or denial prompted me to tell some of the story in this book.

Problems resulting from the interaction of human beings with their environment and each other continually present us with challenges. Now more than at any time in our past, we need to be able to draw on the talents and expertise of all people who possess them. In addition, all human beings have the right to develop their potential and to work toward their own goals. Within this context, it is irrational and unjust deliberately to prevent the full development of any person, female or male.

Patricia J. Thompson

3

When I attended the University of Toronto in the 1950s, I had my first taste of sexual discrimination. I was not allowed to earn money doing summer field work like the male biologists in my class, but instead had to accept low-paying laboratory jobs where I gained little biological experience. To be able to do field research on the giraffe in Africa after my graduation, I had to use only initials in correspondence and thus pretend to be a man.

After I had earned my doctorate and become an assistant professor in zoology at the University of Guelph in 1968, I thought my being hired indicated that sexual discrimination no longer existed in academia. During the next few years, having published 20 refereed papers in zoology, supervised several master's students, and taught a number of courses in which 90 per cent of my students rated me as a good or very good teacher, I assumed that I would be granted tenure. Instead, the head of the department told me that I was unacceptable for permanent employment because I had a family and had to commute to work. At this time a recommendation from the Canadian Association of University Teachers made this assessment of my professional qualifications: "Dr. Dagg has excellent academic credentials. Her list of papers published in refereed journals is more impressive than those of many tenured, promoted staff members" (letter, March 10, 1972). But the university ignored this evidence. I was one of several experienced women professors who were denied tenure at that time, and who watched as men with far less expertise were given it. It is economical to fire an untenured professor every few years and hire a new one at a lower rate of pay, and the department chose to fire women instead of men.

During the next few years of unemployment, I wrote more research papers and wrote alone or with others four books of biology. For International Women's Year in 1975 I was chosen one of the top living women scientists in Canada, and the National Museums of Canada in Ottawa exhibited my work. I felt I had a good chance of being hired at Wilfrid Laurier University when two job openings came up in my areas of research because I had previously taught there successfully as a part-time lecturer. However, the university refused even to interview me. Two men were hired, one of whom had only a master's degree.

When I learned that the better qualified of these two had only a fair teaching record and had published only ten research papers, I asked the Ontario Human Rights Commission to look into this case. The university claimed that the appointee had an international research record. The human rights investigator found that this meant that ten people in the U.S. and Canada had requested reprints of his work. In contrast, 550 people from 30 countries had requested reprints of my research publications. Despite the evidence which seemed to show clearcut discrimination against a woman (me) in favor of a less qualified man, the Ontario Human Rights Commission refused me a board of inquiry. Because I was not satisfied with the commission's decision, I appealed it to a judicial review by the Supreme Court of Ontario, but this court ruled that no one could force the Commission to set a board of inquiry.

I am now fortunate enough to be Academic Director of the Independent Studies Program at the University of Waterloo, a unique program in which students, not faculty, decide not only what they will learn but who shall be hired as academic staff. I have published about 50 research papers in biology and written 10 biological books. I do not have tenure. I hope its lack will not cost me my job when this book is published.

Anne Innis Dagg

Chapter 1
Realities of Student Life

You come in the door . . . equal but having experienced the discrimination — the refusal of professors to take you seriously; the sexual overtures and the like — you limp out doubting your own ability to do very much of anything.

Female PhD student
quoted in Hall and Sandler, 1982

Students are the most important part of a university. In Canada, despite a history of quotas in several disciplines (Zerker, 1987), the number of women students has increased gradually over the years until now there are as many women undergraduates as there are men. Women actually outnumber men in education, fine and applied arts, humanities, agricultural and biological sciences, and in the health professions. In the social sciences, women and men are similar in number, while in mathematics and physical sciences, and in engineering and applied sciences, men far outnumber women (Table 1–1).

Except in engineering and applied sciences, undergraduate women constitute proportionately more of the part-time than of the full-time enrolment (Table 1–1). This seems to be because women are more likely than men to have obligations such as childcare, domestic work, and work in the labor force while they are in university. Some parents still support and encourage a son more than a daughter. Since women have a harder time than men finding well-paid summer jobs and earn less once they graduate, those who have to borrow money for university suffer far more from the burden of debts than do their male counterparts. One single parent who quickly realized that even the maximum amount of funding available under the British Columbia Student Assistance Program ($5900) was not enough to support herself and her two children as well as pay tuition fees and books, gave up custody of her children rather than try to bring them up under the conditions of extreme poverty that student aid and welfare allowed her (*Canadian Federation of Students* newspaper, 1986–87). The five year degree limit of that same student aid program also works against single-parent, usually women, students (*Ubyssey,* University of British Columbia, July 15, 1987).

Part-time students, who are usually women, are further disadvantaged by the fact that they are eligible for fewer bursaries, fellowships, and scholarships than are full-time students. In addition, many programs do not allow part-time students. At Dalhousie University, where there are 6700 full-time students, about half of them women, less than one per cent of the budget goes toward continuing education in which there are 1800 part-time students, two-thirds of whom are women. The director of the Centre of Continuing Studies says that there is resistance within the university community against women students: "Some will still say that you shouldn't educate a woman because she'll only get pregnant or married. Of course, no one wants to say this publicly — it's an insidious form of sexism" (*Kitchener-Waterloo Record,* October 30, 1987; personal communication, December 21, 1987).

Our school systems do not foster the belief that women and men deserve the same chance to achieve what they want in life. Indeed, many teachers speak out against "women's lib" and "radical feminists" to their students. It is therefore not surprising that most university women do not promote feminism, and that they do not examine course material, professors' behavior, or the content of textbooks with a critical eye. When a group of women at the University of Waterloo put up posters asking for sexist or non-sexist comments about these components of the education offered at the university, few students responded, and most or all of those who did were already feminists. The lack of help this group obtained from the administration, and the comments which referred specifically to dozens of professors, however, provide ample evidence that the low response rate did not indicate a lack of sexism at the university. Some of those responses were:

- In a history of law course, "comments made in class with regard to women's status and purpose as seen in the past were completely inappropriate and definitely *not funny* as obviously the professor thought they were. Very insensitive. I left class early on several occasions."
- A geography professor's "rapport with the students is different for females and males. He tends to intimidate the females and make us seem less credible than the males, or ridicules us. He has invaded the personal space of more than one female in the class to the extent where he'll put his arm around her to 'make a point' or do some role-playing which is unnecessary. He makes unnecessary remarks about sexuality, beautiful women, etc."

Table 1-1. Percentage of Enrolled Students Who Are Women in Undergraduate, Master's, and Doctoral Programs — Full-time and Part-time in Eight Fields, 1984–85

	Undergraduate		Master's		Doctorate	
	Full-time	Part-time	Full-time	Part-time	Full-time	Part-time
Education	67.0	71.2	62.3	61.0	50.6	47.5
Fine & Applied Arts	59.9	73.5	56.6	61.3	43.1	53.6
Humanities	59.2	69.9	56.3	56.1	44.1	39.9
Social Sciences	49.3	55.2	42.6	36.5	41.9	36.7
Agricultural & Biological Sciences	54.5	64.3	42.3	44.5	30.3	22.4
Engineering & Applied Sciences	11.9	8.9	11.6	10.4	7.2	4.8
Health Professions	65.7	84.5	60.7	66.8	36.0	41.4
Mathematics & Physical Sciences	27.8	35.9	22.0	22.4	15.2	16.0
Total	48.2	60.5	42.1	45.3	32.6	35.5

— compiled from Statistics Canada, 1986 (Cat. 81-204)

- A sociology professor is "very condescending to all females in class, particularly older women. Calls female students 'dear,' and does everything but pat them on the head. This man is a disaster. Avoid!!"
- An accounting professor told a woman, "I like your chest," pretending that he meant the logo on her T-shirt.
- An engineer who does academic advising tells women who object to his use of sexist language and of sexist imagery in his course that they have no right to do so. "I will not be censored!" he states.
- A mathematics professor told a woman who had written an excellent report that she was "a good girl." This woman has a 17-year-old son.
- A kinesiology professor "makes jokes about women — usually about their inability or personality (stereotype). His jokes are obvious attempts to be funny but I fail to see amusement in jokes about women." The class notes this man wrote used "man" and "mankind" and quoted studies that involved mostly or entirely male subjects.

At the University of Victoria, Joan Graves (1986) sent out nearly 500 questionnaires concerning sex discrimination. When she analyzed the 105 completed questionnaires, she found that all the students noted a dearth of female professors in their disciplines, but that 76 per cent felt this had not affected their academic experience in any way. The respondents agreed that there was little course content by or about women, but most felt this merely reflected social norms. Some students commented that equalizing course content would mean discriminating against men! One woman wrote:

> I really can't see sexism as a problem at UVic except where die-hard feminists see themselves as persecuted . . . and then they are the ones who are creating the problem.

Another noted:

> It is groups like yourselves [Women's Centre and B. C. Public Interest Research Group] which pull women back by giving women a bad name and reminding the majority of humans that perhaps we are not equal. There is no need to even raise that question.

It is evident that most students do not take sexism seriously. Some joke about it — "Maybe I'll get a good mark if I show more cleavage" — some ignore it hoping it will go away, and some don't know it exists. When a reporter asked two senior students at the University of Toronto if they thought being women had hindered them so far, one answered, "It's helped. Quotas. It's easier for us to get into most of the professional schools" (*Toronto*, April, 1987, p. 37). There are no quotas favoring women the way there used to be favoring men and gentiles (Zerker, 1987), but these women sincerely believed otherwise.

Women at university may not feel discriminated against, but they still often censor their behavior. In one class of mature master's students in business at York University, a student noted that men were speaking up in class twice as often as women, even though there were about as many women as men present and the women were doing at least as well as the men. Nor did women speak out more after they had been told about this difference, which would affect marks given for class participation (*Globe and Mail*, August 8, 1987).

There are proportionately fewer women graduate than undergraduate students in every field, and proportionately fewer women enrol in doctoral than in master's programs (Statistics Canada, 1986a). This is especially unfortunate because it is the doctoral students who have a chance to become professors. It is also ironic that in graduate school women students learn not only about their chosen disciplines, but indirectly more and more about "their own inadequacy and lack of authority. The more proficient we become at our lessons, the less likely we are to challenge male dominance" (Spender, 1982, p. 30). Women have little chance ever to become tenured professors, while feminists are even less likely than other women to be hired at all (see Chapter 7). Indeed, many people with PhDs are unable to find any suitable work; 15 per cent of the women who received PhDs from Ontario universities in the spring of 1985 were unemployed a year later, a rate nearly 3 times that of their male counterparts (Ontario Ministry of Education and Ministry of Colleges and Universities, 1987).

Whereas five fields had more women than men at the undergraduate level, only four programs had more women at the master's level, and only one at the doctoral level (Table 1–1). Again, by far the fewest women are in mathematics and physics, and engineering and applied science programs. This lack of women occurs in part because where there are few women there tends to be more prejudice against them; if few women are present in a certain discipline, it has come to seem appropriate that this should be so, and an influx of women seems "wrong" (Simeone, 1987, pp. 10–1).

10

Graduate school is a less attractive option for women than it is for men in part because women are less likely to find good jobs after graduate work, and in part because they have a harder time there. Ella Haley, for her 1985 master's degree at the University of Waterloo, researched the problems of men and women at graduate school in four areas or departments of an Ontario university. She interviewed 39 students in depth about what they were experiencing. A number of the women complained of sexual discrimination by their professors. A life science doctoral candidate said that she didn't feel comfortable with some professors in her department because they made it plain that they thought women were only good for making babies and washing dishes. In this same department, a master's student felt she was at a disadvantage with the professors because she did not drink beer or play sports with them. As well, she felt they were inhibited from telling certain jokes when she was present (which is both good and bad: the student doesn't have to listen to demeaning humor, but she is aware that her presence is viewed negatively). In another department, a master's student who later withdrew from her program said that women were angry and resentful because the male professors refused to admit them into their male "fraternity" (Haley, 1985, p. 56).

Other graduate students Haley interviewed were more specific about professors who harassed them. One woman was questioned about her dress, asked whether or not she was pregnant, and queried about why she was not with her husband who worked out of town. Another woman who won a scholarship was told by a male professor, "Good, now you can buy yourself a husband" (p. 57). At the University of Toronto recently, two women graduates were initially refused employment at the university because they were pregnant (U of T Ombudsman, 1986).

The beleaguered feeling of women graduate students may be so strong that they warn each other about professors who proposition students or have affairs with them. Two professors warned students about their colleagues: "I can't warn you enough about him," "Be careful with him. . . . Watch your ass" (Haley, p. 57). Several students formed a support group, Women in Science and Engineering (WISE), to discuss such issues as well as to meet professional women in their disciplines.

The "hard" sciences and engineering develop and produce technology and materials that affect all of our lives in the most profound ways. These disciplines are perceived as masculine, presumably because they are so scientific and apparently rational. Doctoral candidates are also more likely than those in the arts to complete their degrees (Statistics Canada, 1986a, and see Cude, 1987) and to be awarded more money by a university for doing so (e.g., the science departments of the University of Waterloo give their graduate students $12 000 a year or more, while graduate students in arts receive about half that amount). Because of economic importance of these fields, financial aid to graduates (fellowships, scholarships, research and teaching assistant funds) is more abundant than in the arts, so men are further advantaged by their concentration in heavily funded fields. Their advantage will increase in the years ahead as universities and governments increasingly fund and favor technological research. In Chapter 2, we shall discuss the sexist atmosphere that affronts women in engineering schools and discourages them from studying there.

Haley found that women students in science and engineering were critical about the lack of women professors. One engineer said, "I've never had a woman prof in my discipline. There's only one woman prof I've had and she's not in my discipline. I feel this is very poor" (p. 57). A scientist in a department with only one woman professor said, "They say there aren't that many qualified women, but the point is since I've started here, they have hired at least five profs. None of them have been women and you can't tell me that there aren't [enough qualified women]. One-fifth of the PhDs in this field are women. So why do they hire five to six new profs and not one of them a woman?" (p. 57)

Both women graduate students and women professors have trouble becoming part of the male academic network. Even if a graduate student has a woman professor as a mentor, this may not help her much. Without access to the old boys' network, women scholars

> have fewer opportunities to work collaboratively on research projects. They are less likely to be informed of the latest developments in their fields and to benefit from informal discussion of their ideas and their work. They are less likely to receive career advice and assistance, and have to "learn the ropes" the hard way. They have fewer political allies to lobby for them or their ideas. They have less influence within their departments and have a harder time being heard by their colleagues. Additionally, women are deprived of a sense of community in their work environment and may feel isolated and unsupported. Obviously, enduring even a few of these hardships puts women at a disadvantage. (Simeone, 1987, p. 90)

Some of Haley's sample felt they were not taken seriously by their male peers. One reported that her male classmates had broken into her office and written obscenities on her desk.

Haley found that women, more than men, suffered from stress, especially in their first year of graduate work. They were worried about their academic performance, their interaction (or lack of interaction) with professors and fellow students, and their financial situation. Some also were upset about moving to a new university and about how their studies affected their spouses, partners, or children, if they had these. Those who were single often mentioned loneliness as a problem.

Stress expressed itself in a number of ways: depression and worry, illness, disease, poor diet, "lop-sided lives" with little in them but work, and increased consumption of alcohol, cigarettes, and coffee (p. 85). Feeling less readily accepted than men in graduate school increases women's stress. More drop out, fewer proceed to doctoral studies from master's programs, and many are slow to complete their degrees. Haley found that the graduates who progressed quickly in graduate work had one or more of three characteristics: a proven scholastic ability (through publishing and/or winning a scholarship), a colleague-like relationship with their professors, and self-confidence (p. 141). Each of these characteristics tended to feed the others: if students worked closely with their supervisors, perhaps because of their self-confidence, they were likely to publish more; if their supervisors ignored them they were less likely to publish papers, to win scholarships, or to be self-confident. Women more than men tended to lack self-confidence and a close relationship with their professors.

Haley notes in her paper that the university she studied penalized slow students by such things as reduced funding, which could prevent them from completing their degrees or proceeding on to further ones. She feels that universities should examine their procedures and attitudes toward students to see whether they affect women and men differently. University departments select only the best students for graduate studies; why, then, do so many talented students, often women, do poorly in graduate school? Haley's interviewees themselves indicated the necessity of "game-playing," "ass-kissing," and "rhetoric" (pp. 141–2).

In 1983, the Dean of Graduate Studies at the University of Waterloo presented a report to the University Senate focussing on the "success rate" of women and men graduate students in completing graduate degrees in the preceding five years (p. 143). The success rate was similar for women and men in the Science Faculty, but not in the Arts Faculty. There, significantly more men than women completed master's degrees, and at the doctoral

13

level the men were twice as successful as the women. Could it have been because these data were embarrassing for the university, that this report was soon withdrawn from the public record? Rather than address the difficulties that women experience in graduate school, did the university prefer to conceal the statistics? As Haley found, data which indicate sexist behavior in university departments are routinely unavailable officially and almost impossible to obtain in any other way. Nor have other groups been more open to her research. When she applied to have her findings presented at a 1987 conference on higher education, her paper was judged high in "current or emerging interest," but was refused (letter, December 22, 1987).

Chapter 2
Science and Engineering

The sciences have always been the disciplines considered most masculine, both in the way in which they are conceived and in the overwhelming predominance of male participants, particularly at the upper levels.

Angela Simeone
Academic Women: Working Towards Equality, 1987

In early 1987, an Ontario university wrote to the 2000 women alumni (sic) of its Faculty of Science, noting that they constituted about 33 per cent of the faculty's graduates. The letter asked for employment information from these women so that a careers pamphlet could be prepared "to encourage students by the variety of kinds of work that women graduates have found, but to do so realistically." The letter noted, "Role models are important, and we want our women graduates to be seen and appreciated" (letter, January 9, 1987).

This letter must have caused many of its recipients a hearty laugh. The university has produced thousands of women scientists, many of them at the doctoral level, but it has never hired any of its own women graduates as professors. Nor has it hired more than a handful of women science faculty from any other institution. The university seems to be fostering the "successful women in science" syndrome to give the impression that there is equality of opportunity in science and that any woman can be a successful scientist — if she is good enough. The university can boast about opportunities for women in its pamphlet (after all, a few women *have* been very successful) in order to increase its appeal to potential high school women applicants. It will ignore the fact that sexual discrimination is present in all fields and at all levels of science, making women who study biology or chemistry less likely than men to find employment in science or to be paid anywhere near their male colleagues' salaries. It also overlooks the fact that all universities are loath to hire women professors, no matter how impressive their qualifications.

Women scientists at universities in Canada are few and far between. They make up about eight per cent of faculty members in biology even though as early as 1870 Queen's University deemed this subject a suitable one for women (Neatby, 1978, p. 133). Women comprise about two per cent of professors in chemistry, about one per cent in geology, and about one per cent in physics (*Commonwealth Universities Yearbook,* 1985). The proportion of women who are full professors in each discipline is, of course, much lower than this.

Science is considered a male discipline, and no matter how good a woman scientist is, she is unlikely ever to become a tenured professor. Humanities scholars, including such world-famous figures as Hannah Arendt, Jane Jacobs, Barbara Ward, and Barbara Tuchman, can if necessary work in their homes and in good libraries to write brilliant essays and books. Most scientists, on the other hand, need a laboratory in which to do their research. This costs money which most women cannot get. Occasionally women are allowed university laboratory space, especially if they have a husband on faculty to vouch for them, but they are not paid. Maria Goeppert Mayer worked this way at a U.S. university until she was awarded a Nobel Prize in 1963 for her research on the structure of atomic nuclei. Only then was she offered a paid position.

Other women are less fortunate. At an Ontario university, one scientist who worked for nothing in a research laboratory for 14 years, and who had brought in up to $16 000 in federal grant money each year, decided in 1986 to apply for a paid job through the Excellence Fund, a one-time grant from the Ontario government used by some universities to upgrade the status of their women scholars. Far from being rewarded for her volunteer work, she was refused a position and told that she had been lucky to have been allowed to do any research at all. She fought this ruling for a year, and recently obtained a part-time, limited-term paid position (personal communication, October 14, 1987).

This is the same university whose dean of science told the senior author in 1972 that he would never give tenure to a married woman. He rationalized that married women did not need tenure because their husbands looked after them financially; the fact that no one without tenure can become a permanent professor did not worry him. He later wrote jovially that his comment did not reflect negatively on women: "My own *personal* preference is for female colleagues and employees rather than male any time!" (letter, November 30, 1973). During his lengthy term as dean no woman received tenure and only one woman science professor was hired from among the many women with PhDs who applied for work. One woman had been hired in 1962, along with her mentor, before this man became dean. Since he has retired, further token women have been hired. Eight per cent of the science faculty at this university are now women.

Male science professors like to state airily that few women have trained as scientists, so it is no wonder that there are few women science professors. This position has no basis in fact. Beginning in 1903, when Clara Cynthia Benson earned and was awarded her PhD in physical chemistry at the University of Toronto, 28 of that university's first 30 women PhDs (1903 to 1928) were in the sciences rather than the humanities and arts (Ford, 1985, p. 46). Many women have found in science a way to transcend the social and cultural bonds that limit their freedom.

Although just 160 women from the University of Toronto and the University of Waterloo received PhDs in science, psychology, engineering, and mathematics, many of them have been unable to find permanent work as scientists. When Anne Dagg (1985) sent a questionnaire about their experiences in science to these and 36 other women scientists, she received a stream of horror stories about their careers. Of the 94 scientists who replied, nearly half were aware of having experienced sexual discrimination in their careers, more so in universities than at other institutions. Many had been unable to find any work in science, and one-quarter had retrained, or were willing to retrain, to find a job. Several became physicians, because at least no one could prevent them from working when they became licensed. But even that route is not straightforward. For example, one woman who graduated as a doctor in the 1960s when she was 42 was told by her dean that she was too old to practise medicine. He helped her find a research job at a hospital, but to get ahead there she was told she needed a PhD, which she then earned. The hospital later dismissed her from the research job which she had held for 11 years. She wrote on her questionnaire, "I felt very depressed when I was tossed out of [the hospital] when in my 50s. It took a long time to get over it." She then, at last, began to practise medicine, at which she makes enough money to finance her own research.

Many male professors and others feel not only that there are few women scientists, but that those few are unlikely to be committed workers. They reiterate that scientists cannot take off time to raise a family, as they imply women would tend to do. Not only does this attitude force women to choose between children and a career, a "choice" no man must ever face, but it does not reflect the facts of women scientists' lives. Of the women who answered Dagg's questionnaire, a few were raising children and working part-time, but 74 per cent had worked steadily, usually full-time, since they received their doctorates. Those who had a gap in their work record had often been unable to find work for some period of time. The number of women PhDs in science has been increasing rapidly (Table 2–1), creating additional scientists desperate to find work, but universities have had few openings for science professors, male or female, since the early 1970s.

During the late 1970s, many university scientists in Canada began to push for more graduate students, arguing that without them, the scientific community in the future would suffer. As Dr J. K. Morton, Chairperson of the Biology Department at the University of Waterloo, wrote: "Any suggestion that this country is overproducing PhDs in the biological sciences is nonsense; we are not. The jobs are there but qualified Canadians to fill them are not" (University of Waterloo *Gazette,* January 4, 1978). The Biological Council of Canada predicted: "Over the next 5 to 10 years career opportunities for scientists at the doctoral level will be highly competitive and insufficient to meet the demand" (1978). In the same year Dr W. G. Henry, head of the Metallurgical Engineering Department at Queen's University, wrote that more PhDs should be produced (*Science Forum*, November–December, 1978). And P. A. Larkin of the Institute of Animal Resource Ecology at the University of British Columbia feared that "by 1985 Canada could be shopping again abroad for scientists because the number entering PhD programs now is declining" (letter of November 7, 1978).

This annoyed many women scientists who had been trying for years to find work. Dagg and a colleague, who both felt that many professors were interested more in having research done under their direction by poorly paid graduate students than in the future careers of these students, founded in 1978 a lobbying group of unemployed/underemployed Canadian doctoral scientists. About 20 scientists who were unable to find permanent work in their disciplines contacted the group. Some had turned to other fields, training as teachers and librarians; some were working at short-term, poorly paid post-doctoral positions; and others were without work, or working part-time and/or in other disciplines. One woman biologist, who had unsuccessfully written to over 100 institutions and companies requesting work, had finally accepted a post-doctoral research job that paid far less than graduates with bachelor's degrees received in other fields.

Although some trained men were unable to find suitable scientific work in the late 1970s, most of our contacts were women; there were many fewer women than men scientists with PhDs, yet women were disproportionately more likely than men to be

Table 2–1. Percentage of Canadian Doctoral Degrees in Science Awarded to Women or of Women Enrolled in PhD Programs

Discipline	1969-70[1]		1975[2]		1984[3]	
	Total Number of PhDs Awarded	Percentage Awarded to Women	Total Number of PhDs Awarded	Percentage Awarded to Women	Total Enrolment of PhD Programs	Percentage of Women Enrolled
Biology	126	10	159	17	858	29
Chemistry and Biochemistry	240	3	197	13	987	22
Geology	37	0	34	3	306	18
Physics	123	4	108	4	532	7

[1]From Statistics Canada, 1971
[2]From Statistics Canada, 1977
[3]From Statistics Canada, 1986

19

un/underemployed. In the early 1970s many reports were produced showing that few women scientists had been hired at various Canadian universities, but little was done by these universities. In 1977, when only three per cent of the Science Faculty of the University of Waterloo were women and when the vice-president indicated he was actively seeking women to hire, a highly qualified woman who applied for an advertized job was turned down without an interview in favor of a man. Indeed, whereas in Canada 4.7 per cent of the faculty were women in the mathematical and physical sciences in 1965–66, their percentage had decreased in 1975–76 to only 3.6 per cent (Symons and Page, 1984, p. 193). Nor are other groups supportive to women scientists; for example, U.S. women physicists experience five times as much unemployment as their male counterparts, are paid less, and work in positions of lesser rank (Branscomb, 1979, p. 75), whereas the suicide rate for women chemists is five times that of white American women as a whole (Simeone, 1987, p. 12). Currently, many academics and the media are talking again about a "brain drain" of Canadian scientists because some professors have taken jobs outside Canada. This attitude ignores the many women and young scientists, currently wasting their training, who would love to replace them and bring new enthusiasm and insights to university teaching and research. They would cost the universities far less money, as well.

Many science faculties across Canada claim that they are doing all they can to encourage girls to study science, but they have little grasp of how such encouragement might be undertaken. For example, one university sends a physics test to over 5000 top high school science and math students across Canada each year. Women have often complained that these tests are heavily sex-biased, giving girls the impression that physics is a masculine subject, but the university refuses to change the type of questions asked. The 1987 test had problems involving 20 males but only 3 females — Jane (swinging down to Tarzan), Mother Bear (of the Three Bears), and Wonderwoman. I would take no effort at all to portray ordinary girls and women doing active things, but the physicists refuse to consider this.

Would science be different if there were more women in it? Many people think it would. At present, science is a macho discipline with cutthroat competition between laboratories struggling each to be first to discover something new. Women have been socialized to get along with other people, so women scientists, if they could, might work in co-operation to develop new scientific theories and ideas. As well, women might ask different questions than men when deciding what issues to address. They might not work to answer the question, "How can we win the next war?" but rather address the question, "How can we ensure that the world has peace?" Such possibilities can only arise when we have thousands more women scientists in the work force, and hundreds more in positions of real power.

The natural science most popular among women is biology, which is more closely related to other people and animals than are disciplines such as physics and chemistry; young girls who love to watch and care for domestic and wild animals may develop a deep interest in these creatures and how they function without being seen as unfeminine. About half of university biology students are now women (Statistics Canada, 1986a), even though only eight per cent of their professors are women (Dagg, 1985, p. 69).

Despite the large number of women who are keenly interested in biology, the subject has been defined and explored almost entirely by men, who have viewed this discipline from a male perspective. Sexism pervades both the constructs of biology and its language, which devalues what is female compared to what is male (as Alcock, 1984). Such comparisons are also used for women. It is claimed that since female non-human animals are portrayed as less aggressive/more submissive/more passive than males, then it is only natural that women, too, should follow this pattern. Recent feminist research has shown that females are often more aggressive, sometimes dominant, and usually more active than males, but this knowledge is generally ignored in mainstream biology texts and courses (Dagg, 1983).

Instead, current textbooks and articles talk about males and their harems as if the males somehow own females and breeding rights, which they do not; about females that "submit" to males during mating, when in virtually every species it is the female that decides when mating will occur; and about other "feminine" behavior of animals, behavior that men have decided is appropriate to females and therefore "must" occur. It is no accident that these behaviors serve to reinforce male power and female submission (Dagg, 1983).

The new field of sociobiology is notorious for using such language and for comparing the behavior of non-human animals with that of people. Beginning with E. O. Wilson (1975), sociobiologists have developed hypotheses that restrict the human potentials of groups such as women and homosexuals by claiming that their inferior place in society is caused not by societal oppression but by their genetic inheritance. This is a frightening concept with no basis in fact that is being taught each year to many thousands of university students across Canada.

One of the sciences *least* tolerant of women is engineering or applied science. Almost no women ventured into this field until recently, although at present about ten per cent of undergraduate engineers are women. Considering that there are almost no female professors, that course material is accompanied by sexist jokes and language, and that the students organize to produce notorious sexist newspapers and stag parties, it is surprising that *any* female students dare to apply to engineering schools. A prime survival tactic of those who do enter engineering is to identify with their male peers; most of them keep their opinions about sexism to themselves or agree with the men engineers that sexism is unimportant and that feminists who object to it have no sense of humor.

Although women have been lobbying for years for more women engineering professors, few have been hired. Indeed, the University of Calgary recently refused to hire its adjunct assistant professor Aleksandra Vinogradov for a Department of Civil Engineering faculty position, even though there is not one woman faculty member holding a tenure-track position in the entire Faculty of Engineering (Grassick, 1987). The Queen's Bench of Alberta has found that the university violated principles of fundamental justice in its hiring process, a decision that the university is still appealing. That a university would rather acquire a reputation for discrimination and spend many thousands of dollars in legal fees than hire one woman engineering professor speaks volumes about its priorities.

The chance that women working within a faculty of engineering will change things for women is slim. The few women in engineering have had to resign themselves to things as they are in order to be accepted. In the fall of 1986, Trudi Collins, a reporter from *Otherwise*, interviewed Jane Phillips, the only woman professor in the Department of Chemical Engineering at the University of Toronto. Professor Phillips was quick to insist that she is not a feminist. She told Collins firmly what women have been told for centuries: "As long as you are good enough you will get ahead. The point is to take advantage of these hiring procedures and then prove yourself." She said, "It may take a woman longer [than a man] to rise on the career ladder," but did not comment that in her department she was the *only* woman even *on* this ladder (*Otherwise,* November 25, 1986).

The misogynist atmosphere in engineering does not worry Professor Phillips. When Collins asked about her feeling toward the engineering newspaper, *The Toike*, she replied, "When I was an undergrad, the jokes were off-color but funny, now they're just obscene and not funny at all. Who really reads [*The Toike*] anyway?" However, she was forced to admit that women might be handicapped because of their gender: "The men may not appreciate the competition that the women provide. Indeed, the men can make life very difficult for women they feel don't conform to what they perceive as the woman's role."

Chapter 3
Arts, Law, and Medicine

When students come to learn about economics or sociology (or language, literature, education, psychology, philosophy, political science, anthropology, science) they are taught about men, and men's view of the world, and this is a lesson in male supremacy. While on the one hand women have achieved some success in gaining entry to education, it is entry to men's education and it serves to reinforce male supremacy and control in our society.

Dale Spender
Invisible Women: The Schooling Scandal, 1982

Recent feminist research indicates how all-pervasively our knowledge of human history and affairs has been biased against women. This bias has been so complete that if women try to redress the balance by adding feminist content or perspective to a discipline, they may be accused angrily of trying to distort the body of knowledge. As one professor of literature stated the week before this book went to press, "Women? What do we need women for? We have a discipline of the greatness of all humanity: Shakespeare, Dickens, Shaw, all of them. They include women. To bring in women *qua* women is to destroy human achievement" (personal communication, February 7, 1988).

In almost all mainstream arts courses taught in universities across Canada, the content that the professor presents is the content that the students must accept and learn. If they do not learn it, they will fail. There is no acknowledgement that the information presented is only a sample of all possible information that could be presented, and that it is usually professors, almost always male, who have decided what is the accepted body of knowledge in each discipline. This knowledge is used in turn to reinforce social relations already present in society. Needless to say, perhaps, information about women is rare in most courses, and information presented from a woman's perspective even more scarce. If students want high marks in some courses, they must be willing to accept with good grace both the absence of information that they might find of central interest, and the biased information presented by professors unwilling to read and accept new research results being published by feminists in every discipline. A university education is expensive for every student; yet women have to pay as much as men, even though their education distorts their vision and undermines their integrity. Women who have earned university degrees have had to accept a male-biased view of the world that will affect them for the rest of their lives. To illustrate the ways in which sexism distorts university teaching, we have chosen examples from a variety of disciplines related to the arts.

Stereotypically, many people think of the fine arts as a feminine discipline, but this is so only if one considers the students taking it in universities. In fine art departments of Ontario universities, about 61 per cent of undergraduate, 56 per cent of master's, and 62 per cent of doctoral students are women, while only 20 per cent of the faculty are women (Groarke, 1983, p. 14).

In universities across Canada, only 17 per cent of professors in art departments are women, and very few of them have any power (*Commonwealth Universities Yearbook,* 1985). The percentage of women professors seems to be increasing slowly, but at the present rate a balance of female and male faculty members will be achieved only in the year 2040 (Sasha McInnes, writing in 1980 as McInnes-Hayman).

The history of discrimination against women art students goes back a long way, as feminist artist Sasha McInnes (1980) found when she analyzed 318 questionnaires submitted by professional women artists, two-thirds of whom had attended art college or university, and 92 per cent of whom had had fewer than 10 per cent women teachers. Most of these women (79 per cent) felt that formal art training had been beneficial, but most also were of two minds. Seventy-three per cent mentioned discouragement from male professors of the type, "Too bad you're a female, but you can paint as a hobby after you're married." One University of Calgary artist wrote, "During the first year I was told blankly that women have no place in art. After declaring my determination and feminist leanings I found encouragement from a few male professors." Another respondent wrote, "When my male professors told me women could not handle careers as well as family responsibilities, all I had to do was look at my female professors who seemed to be doing well at both" (pp. 12–13).

One of Maryon Kantaroff's (1975, p. 11) professors said that there was no point taking women students seriously because none would ever become professional, although in reality all of her female contemporaries but one did go on to become professional sculptors. During her postgraduate studies, all the professors of sculpture were men and most of the models, chosen by the professors, were women. Such models are sometimes treated as sex objects both by students, who make comments about their unsuitability because of their bodily imperfections, and by instructors, who direct models to remain unclothed longer than is necessary, or to strike poses which emphasize their bodies as sex objects.

The preponderance of male art teachers also means that in order to be considered good enough to continue, women must deny their own perspective and use a male bias. The male dominance of university art departments reflects the male dominance of the entire art establishment. If critics are virtually always male, or have a male bias, then it is no wonder that women's art is considered marginal at best. When Vancouver sculptor Persimmon Blackbridge was in art school, she realized that to be accepted she had to make at least one figure of a man for every three female figures. Now she does sculptures of men when she has something to say about men; otherwise she sculpts women because she is a woman and women are her main political focus (personal communication, June 26, 1986).

Some artists in McInnes's sample expressed anger that the art history courses, even if they were taught by a woman, lacked significant information on women artists of the past (McInnes, 1980, p. 13). Without such information, one noted, she was unable to find a context for her work. Another grieved for the lost women she could learn nothing about. This ignorance of past women artists is predictable, given the blatant sexual bias of art history and of the art world. The two most widely used Canadian art history texts perpetuate this sexism and ignorance. J. Russell Harper notes in *Painting in Canada: A History* (1977), a volume of 463 pages, that "it has been my intention to present as thorough as possible a survey of the artists and movements that have contributed to the rich and varied heritage of painting in Canada," and that he had made "efforts to maintain proper perspective and balance throughout" (p. vii). Yet Harper does not include among his 327 artists the second woman to become an academician in the Royal Canadian Academy — Marion Long. He also leaves out or glosses over other fine artists such as Anne Savage, Sarah Robertson, Lillian Freiman, Paraskeva Clark, Joyce Wieland, Rita Letendre, and Betty Goodwin. Nor does Dennis Reid do much better in *A Concise History of Canadian Painting* (1973).

These books are the two most widely used Canadian text and reference books, yet as McInnes points out in her detailed analysis of them, they give a "gross under-representation of Canadian women artists . . . in written material as well as in illustration" (1981, p. 11). The text dealing with women occupies 7 per cent and 10 per cent respectively of the books. Women are rarely considered even in the contemporary period, when women artists have been at least as numerous as male artists. Even fewer pictures by women than mention of them are included in these books, and still fewer women's paintings are in color (1% and 3%) than in black and white (4% and 4% respectively). These and many texts that so blatantly misrepresent women's achievements not only fail half the population, they are dangerous.

Sasha McInnes writes that because of the pronounced skewing against women in art history texts,

> Drastic remedial measures will be necessary to even attempt to undo the damage done to our cultural heritage in general and to women in particular by the invisibility of women artists. The addition of a few elective women's studies courses . . . will be insufficient as a corrective measure. I suggest that representation of Canadian women artists be included in current art history courses where they can be seen by this generation of art students as *natural phenomena* and not as exotic house plants. (1981, p. 14)

Students who take courses on Canadian art might well expect to receive an overview of what all Canadian artists have accomplished in their time. Instead, students are overwhelmingly likely to learn only about Canadian men's art, and about Emily Carr's work and life — including some of her behaviors which, although they were creative survival measures, when taken out of context appear eccentric at best. Students learn nothing of the well over 100 women whose work has been included in foreign exhibitions, despite all the new data about them that is being collected. They learn nothing of the hundreds more women who did and do contribute to the cultural life of this country. To the professors, Canada's art is Canadian men's art. Students learn that, with one exception, women artists were and are of no importance. Women who want to be great artists learn that this is impossible.

A feminist psychology is essential if women are ever to have equality with men, yet the term "feminist psychology" is almost a contradiction in terms: feminism is concerned with equality for women and men, while psychology sees human beings from a male perspective. Jeri Dawn Wine (1982, p. 86) writes, "In challenging the individualistic models of man that underlie psychology, feminist psychology challenges the very underpinnings of male-dominated society."

Wine notes that "there are certain central features of male-stream psychology that render it a particularly barren and hostile environment for the growth of feminist work" (p. 69). One such feature is the scientific approach which may champion male values while masquerading behind the facade of "rationality" and "objectivity." It usually deals not with individuals, but with group averages that remove any personalization of the data. Wine feels that research must become more flexible, with researcher and researched collaborating together to increase human knowledge. Another stumbling block is the excessive energy psychology expends to prove that men and women are different, and that men are superior. It is paradoxical that despite the purported differences between women and men, well over two-thirds of human research has been done only on men, yet has been generalized to include all human beings and is interpreted as information on the whole species, not half of it (p. 70).

Textbooks published for use in general psychology courses indicate that these courses contain little or no material of special interest to women. Many students take psychology at university because they want to know more about their own behavior; women students must feel non-plussed when they realize that topics that affect them and their friends in the most vital ways are not even addressed in their weighty psychology textbooks. In six general psychology texts, all over 580 pages and all published in the 1980s, Dagg (1988) found not a single reference in the index to abortion, battering or beating of wives, or incest. Only one of the six books listed entries on lesbianism, rape, or violence and pornography, all of which were superficial and short. There has been a large amount of feminist research recently on each of these subjects, but it has been ignored in these texts.

Such professorial intransigence leaves some women students in a quandary. They know that the image of women that professors put forward frequently has little to do with their own lives and realities. They know from reading that aggression is often correlated in animals with size rather than sex; female hyenas and female hamsters, for example, are both bigger than their males, and both are more aggressive too. If an exam question asks about aggression, should they answer it with what they know to be true from current research? Or should they give back what the professor has pronounced as the truth, even though they know his "truth" is biased, if not actually wrong? Ambitious students par rot the professor's truth, because they need high marks if they want to go to graduate school.

Sixty years ago, English was not considered an important academic discipline. When Elizabeth Longford, the noted biographer was at Oxford, she was persuaded by her male colleagues to switch from the study of English to that of the classics — Latin and Greek. "English was for women," she writes. She wanted "to tackle a 'man's' subject" (1986, p. 49). Novelist Evelyn Waugh agreed with her, noting that the English school was reserved for "women and foreigners" and thus unworthy of the attention of English gentlemen (Kahan, 1985, p. 3).

English may have been looked down upon, but jobs are jobs; all English professors in the past were men, and most continue to be men. Most English department heads (87 per cent) in Canadian universities are also men (*Canadian Association of Chairmen* [sic] *of English Newsletter,* November, 1987), and they generally hire men in preference to women.

Male-dominated English departments spread their male bias to their students, the clear majority of whom (69 per cent) are women. Books studied in regular English courses are by men far more often than by women. In none of the 1984–85 Canadian university calendars that listed writers to be studied in their course descriptions were women more than a third of those metioned, and usually there were far fewer (Dagg, 1986, p. 39). The widely used *Norton Anthology of English Literature* (4th Edition) has *no* writings by women. In response to women's complaints, Norton published in 1985 a 2457-page book of English literature by women (Gilbert and Gubar, 1985). This book is used in women's studies courses but is not considered comparable to the men's book; "women's literature" remains marginalized in women's studies; "literature" still means men's literature.

Male-oriented professors (including a significant proportion of the few existing women teachers, who know that tenure and promotion depend on pleasing their male colleagues) have an influence that extends far beyond university campuses. Bruce Powe (1981) has noted the large number of university teachers who are also important literary figures in Canada. Publishers often ask professors to assess manuscripts to determine if they are worth publishing; academics

are in the position of being able to tell a captive audience of students which books to buy, which books to read. Their decisions thereby become self-fulfilling prophecies. They decide not only which books meet the "standard of excellence" necessary for publication, but as reviewers and as teachers they control the fate of the books they have chosen. (Nelson, 1982, p. 79)

In part because professors are inclined to choose and promote men's rather than women's work, many more Canadian books by men than women are published (69 per cent by men in 1985), with substantial financial support from Canadian taxpayers via the Canada Council. This is true even though more women than men are serious writers, judging both by the membership of the Writers' Union of Canada (which is about half women) and the Canadian Authors Association (which is two-thirds women) (Dagg, 1986, p. 28), and by the quality of their publications.

With publishers their friends and mentors, professors are far more likely than other people to have their own work published, even though it seems unlikely that creative writers are found significantly more often in academe than elsewhere. For example, when J. Michael Yates of the University of British Columbia was asked by the in-house Sono Nis Press to edit a book to be entitled *Contemporary Poetry of British Columbia* (1970), 19 of the 54 contributors he chose were teaching at universities; 18 of these 19 poets were men (25 per cent of the contributors to the book were women). As another example, in *The Alberta Diamond Jubilee Anthology* (Chalmers, 1979), an analysis of the short biographies of the 111 contributors (33 per cent women) shows that 26 of the contributors are professors, while 15 of the contributors have won awards. Of the professors, 8 per cent are women; of the award winners, 67 per cent are women. It seems that men had a good chance of being included in this volume, edited by a university teacher, if they were also university teachers; women were likely to be included if they were renowned authors who had won awards for their writing.

History has been sensibly defined as "what men have done in public." In history classes, for example, many lectures are devoted to describing when various categories of men won the right to vote. In *The Illustrated History of Canada* (1987), Peter Waite discusses at length the politics of representation by population, but does not mention that the female half of the population was excluded from population, making "rep. by pop." meaningless in reality (pp. 315–318). Scholars writing about current events continue to discuss the possibility of having "one man one vote" in South Africa, as if women do not even exist and need not be considered. Despite history's emphasis on suffrage, women have been much less personally affected by the vote than by such things as gaining control of their fertility and being able to prevent the loss of their children to malnutrition and disease. For many North American women, the frontier a hundred years ago was not the north-west, but the cities where they might go and find paid work. According to most history texts, such matters are not significant.

In another example, Canadian history articles and books written by feminists (such as Sylvia Van Kirk, 1983) discuss the importance of Native women during the early days. They married and/or provided homes for many of the fur traders, were vital in negotiations between Native tribes and voyageurs, and took a leading role in many exploratory expeditions. Without their presence, Canadian history would not be what it is. Such information is all too often ignored or glossed over when non-feminists teach about Canadian history. Pierson and Prentice write:

> With the exception of women's history courses — and these are still rare and taught mainly by women on the fringes of academia — the history curriculum at all levels is still heavily biased towards the traditional. Potential feminist historians are therefore deprived of opportunity in numerous ways; as a result, women are denied their history. . . . Feminist historians feel pressed on every side, nevertheless, not least by the fact so many students of history continue to question the very validity of their enterprise. (1982, pp. 114, 115)

Questioning is not always all that happens. In one U.S. women's history class, several male students refused to allow discussion to take place "by joking and chatting, and generally trying to create an atmosphere around the table to reflect their attitude that this course was irrelevant to their education." They stopped only when a Black woman slammed her fist on the table and demanded they pay attention (Bezucha, 1985, p. 89).

Philosophy, and the general acceptance of certain philosophical concepts, influences our lives far more than most people realize. Virtually all philosophers acknowledged as such in our society have been men, who spoke as men, to men, about men. Women philosophers necessarily engage in a male–female relationship, and thus a sexual and political one, whereas men philosophers do not (Finn, 1982). What is a woman philosopher to make of Aristotle's writing, which relegates women and slaves to servile functions because of their "intrinsic" nature? Phenomenology is problematic because male consciousness is assumed to be the same as consciousness in general; one's consciousness must reflect one's everyday experience, yet philosophical consciousness is male, chauvinistic and oppressive of women. If philosophy weren't so completely a male discipline, it would examine fully issues as fundamental as reproduction and birth (which have been seen as too female to address) and cogitate less on those such as death (which men as well as women experience).

Geraldine Finn summarizes that women are largely excluded from philosophy not only because of its biased perspective, but by intimidation (many male philosophers do not like female philosophers and make their dislike known); by negation (women are considered unsuited for the discipline); by discrimination (women aren't viewed as possible philosophers), or by rejection (at present it is necessary to speak like a man to be a philosopher). Despite this negativity, much feminist philosophy is being published (see, for example, Maureen Ford, et al., Women and Philosophy, *Resources for Feminist Research,* September, 1987).

Social work, which grew out of charities and volunteer assistance to the needy, has traditionally been a female occupation. It still functions largely through women, who comprise 66 per cent of the membership of the Canadian Association of Social Workers (*Canadian Encyclopedia,* 1985). More women than men study social work at every level, to the extent that four-fifths of undergraduate students and 63 per cent of doctoral students are women (Table 3–1). In keeping with this predominance of women professionals, women form most of the part-time practicum or field instructors for social work schools across Canada. They teach students how to deal with actual cases of such things as family disruption, alcoholism, and deviant behavior. For the University of Toronto, the calendar shows that 75 per cent of field instructors are women, while at Wilfrid Laurier University, 63 per cent of the practicum instructors are women.

In contrast with these front line worker/teachers, the full-time faculty in social work schools is largely (61 per cent) made up of men (Table 3–2). Ninety-one per cent of the full professors are men (*Commonwealth Universities Yearbook,* 1987). Most of the male professors have degrees in social work, but analysis of the calendars of ten social work schools indicates that significantly more men than women have been parachuted in as experts from male-dominated fields such as economics, psychology, and administration. The direction in which schools of social work decide to go, and the decisions they take which influence the profession as a whole, are determined primarily by men, and sometimes men who are not even themselves social workers.

Although recently many women have expressed the need for more women professors of social work, as of virtually every other discipline, schools of social work have responded reluctantly if at all. For example, at Laurentian University in 1985 there were ten professors of social work, eight men and two women. One would have hoped this department would have been concerned about the lack of women. Instead, when a position became open and a highly qualified woman applied, she was turned down in favor of a man. One of the two women subsequently left Laurentian because of its anti-woman stance (personal communication, February 3, 1988).

Table 3–1. Student Enrolments in Social Work Programs in Canadian Universities, 1984–85

	Full-time Students		Part-time Students	
	Number of Students	Percentage of Students Who are Women	Number of Students	Percentage of Students Who are Women
Undergraduate	4412	81	2414	79
Master's	877	76	663	69
Doctoral	33	70	21	52

— compiled from Statistics Canada, 1986 (Cat. 81-204)

Table 3–2. Percentage of Full-time Faculty Who are Women in Canadian Schools of Social Work

University	Total Number of Professors	Percentage of Professors Who are Women
University of British Columbia	18	39
Carleton University	12	33
Dalhousie University	21	48
University of Manitoba	29	34
McGill University	23	70
Memorial University	13	31
University of Regina	15	33
University of Toronto	22	32
Wilfrid Laurier University	15	27
University of Windsor	16	25
Total	184	39

— compiled from the *Commonwealth Universities Yearbook,* 1987

Women have encountered similar inequities in other social sciences. One is anthropology, where mainstream research has found men dominant and women subordinate, even though this may not reflect the true status of the sexes (see Tiffany, 1979). At best it is a simplification, since status varies within different families in a tribe, with marital state, and with age: an unmarried woman has less status than a married one in many but not all cultures, and although old women are little valued in the West, they often have high status in other societies.

In economics, work done by women, even when it constitutes the source of food, is usually not taken into account. United Nations statistics show that women's work in the Himalayan region includes 70 per cent of the agricultural work, in Africa, 60–80 per cent, and in other developing countries, at least 50 per cent of the food production, "but this is not included in the economic analysis. *When the same jobs are performed by men, they count as work*" (Spender, 1982, p. 26). Housework is unacknowledged in the same way, although it may involve a woman's energy and time for the whole of her life, and makes possible the work done by those who are dependent on a wife or mother.

For sociology, Margrit Eichler (1985) mentions a number of areas that badly need a feminist perspective — social policy, so that it considers not only men and the family, but women as a distinct group; theories concerning the social division of labor, to show this is a cultural, not a biological, construct; and analyses into sexual violence against women, which is now known to be driven by aggression and hate, not sexuality. One recent study concerns the reproductive functions of women and men. Eichler notes that "Mary O'Brien (1981) has built an entire theory around this issue, concluding that patriarchy can be understood as a male reaction to the insecurity of their contributions to the reproductive process" (Eichler, p. 626). Another area of concern to feminist sociologists is the ever-growing control of male doctors and researchers over women's bodies, control that increases drastically as men perfect technologies that take the processes of conception and childbirth away from women and into the realm of high (male) technology.

Law

The male bias learned in law school is evident in the courts of Canada. One judge continued to sit on the bench for many years after he was known to treat women in a sexist way. He ordered

34

them to go back to physically abusive spouses because the Bible stated they should be subservient to their husbands. He was fired in 1987 (*Globe and Mail,* January 16, 1987). Women lawyers specializing in criminal law have been called "girl" by a judge, have had their hands caressed by a judge during consultation, and have been addressed as "gentlemen" because a judge refused to acknowledge them as women (*Globe and Mail,* April 11, 1987). In cases of rape, the debate in court may still centre not on the alleged rapist and his actions, but on the character of the victim.

Although over two-fifths of law students are now women, traditionally law remains an overwhelmingly male-dominated discipline and there have been, and continue to be, few women law professors. In 11 universities across Canada, only 12 per cent of law professors are women (*Commonwealth Universities Yearbook,* 1985). This means that law is taught from a man's point of view. If women hired to teach law try to change this, as Sheila McIntyre did when she joined the faculty at Queen's University in the fall of 1985, they have a difficult, if not impossible, task. McIntyre was anxious to address "male-defined and male-centred models of legal discourse, thought, doctrine, process, professionalism and education" so that women's interests, experiences, and perspectives would no longer be excluded and devalued in the classroom, in the profession, and in society at large (1987, p. 7). She wanted to teach in a classroom where women's concerns mattered and where women students would feel free to express themselves.

When McIntyre put her ideas into practice, there were two major confrontations in her classes. These were triggered by her use of non-sexist language in her lectures (i.e., "he or she" instead of the exclusive "he," and "women and men" instead of "men") which male students considered to be "shoving [her] politics down students' throats," and the consideration of legal points from a woman's perspective (p. 7).

Half a dozen men resented discussion of gender bias in law. During the class they were deliberately disruptive, unco-operative, and angry. They tried to prevent students who disagreed with their point of view from speaking by insulting and interrupting them. When McIntyre tried to legitimize the opinions of other students, they were abusive to her, too. One man shouted at her that the questions she had asked were irrelevant and a waste of time.

After this class, several feminists told MacIntyre that they were very distressed. They no longer felt they could safely speak in her class, and that even if they did so and McIntyre validated their viewpoint, they were worred that McIntyre would be subject to more abuse from the male students. Their concern was well-founded, for shortly after this a man who claimed to represent the abusive men in her course announced how these men wanted material taught and discussed, and presented the ultimatum that if McIntyre did not want to be attacked in future, she should not raise the issue of gender again (p. 7).

The second confrontation occurred in McIntyre's seminar on labor. She encouraged those students who were usually silent to speak, but when they did so, expressing an alternative point of view to that generally accepted, their ideas were attacked by several male students. These students interrupted, laughed, or talked over other students who wanted to discuss the alternative, insisting that conflict is unavoidable in law, as in life, and that alternatives could not be considered. Following this seminar, women in the course told McIntyre that they were too intimidated to speak in class and one asked if she could substitute an extra paper for that portion of her grade based on class participation (p. 18).

Discussions on gender were held in McIntyre's courses during the rest of the year, and tensions remained (p. 18). McIntyre became widely known as a feminist, and because of this had to deal both with anti-feminist professors and students, and with feminists who were appalled at the sexism in the law school. She had at least two dozen visits from women students who found remarks from a total of nine professors to be sexist and offensive and/or whose concerns about gender issues had been trivialized. Queen's University, and undoubtedly all Canadian law faculties, have a long way to go if they are to teach non-biased course material in a manner in which both women and men students can participate fully in class.

In 1987, Osgoode Hall Law School at York University decided to pick as its new dean not the current associate dean, Mary Jane Mossman, whom many people expected would be promoted, but a man brought in from outside the university. Osgoode has never had a woman dean. Thousands of women found this a profoundly tragic decision and a missed opportunity for both women and the law; 124 women have launched a complaint of systemic sex discrimination with the Ontario Human Rights Commission (*Globe and Mail*, September 29, 1987). The president of York University supported the new man, agreeing with the selection committee that "Osgoode really needed a shot of adrenalin from a new perspective." Mossman noted that instead, "An insider was actually chosen. There is a whole stream in feminist literature that suggests the real outsiders, the real people with new ideas, are women"(*Globe and Mail,* June 4, 1987). If Osgoode Hall had wanted the fresh perspective of an outsider, it would have chosen a woman.

Medicine

The largely male medical profession has caused problems for women ever since men wrested power away from the wise women traditional healers and from the midwives who helped deliver babies. Until very recently, male doctors viewed menstruation, pregnancy, and menopause as physical diseases; young girls are still advised to have babies rather than to study; and women were (and are) subjected to needless hysterectomies, untested drugs, and reckless experimentation (Ehrenreich and English, 1979, p. 140). Male doctors have applied the same biases to the few women who joined their ranks as they have to their female patients.

Although women doctors have been trained in Canada for over one hundred years, women in medicine have far to go. Students have still to put up with overt sexism, as the following examples show:

- To a clinical group of five men and one woman, the male clinician begins rounds each day with, "Gentlemen, shall we begin." The group ignored this until one day a male student pointed out that one of them was a woman. The professor replied, "You could have fooled me — she has no tits."
- A teacher constantly patronizes his women students by referring to them as "honey" and "love."
- A male professor refuses to recognize questions from, or to allow participation by, women in his class.
- A professor announces that women doctors are a menace because, unlike their male colleagues, they insist on caring for their sick children.
- A presentation on the contribution of doctors to society features a slide depicting a woman with bare breasts which look like cones of vanilla ice cream.
- A male teacher is offered a Christmas gift by male members of his class: a strip-tease performed by a female stripper which was to be videotaped and later showed to other classes. (Support Group, 1985, pp. 63–4)

Women students who challenge such sexist behavior have to contend with their student colleagues, who ask why they are being so fussy and why they can't take a joke. They must also face their sexist professors, who may judge them troublemakers who will not fit easily into a working team and/or who merit low marks.

One of the reasons that medical schools can continue to be so misogynistic is that there are few women professors (Table 3–3). Some have more women teachers than others, but their numbers are far below the proportion of women students.

Many more women are now being admitted to medical school than were formerly, but 57 per cent of medical students are still male, and women have much better chance of acceptance in some medical schools than others (Table 3–4).

The University of Toronto "Murmurs of the Heart" Workshop discussed many of the problems that are still before women at Canadian medical schools (Support Group, 1985). First among these is the male-dominated power structure, where there is little impetus for change that would benefit women. Yet women would like a number of changes.

Women medical students would like to be able to choose freely their area of specialization. At present, women are likely to become family physicians, pediatricians, psychiatrists, and community health workers. These disciplines are seen as suitably low-key, feminine ones concerned with children, mental health, and society. Male-dominated residency programs such as surgery, orthopedics, urology, and obstetrics and gynecology are difficult for women to enter. They may even lack change rooms, washrooms, and surgical garb for women trainees.

The training schedule for would-be doctors was set up for men by men. For women who have children to look after or households to care for, such a schedule is horrendous, and may be impossible. Many find the excessive work-load carried in hospitals by interns to be not only oppressive for women, but destructive for men too. There seems no need to have interns on call for long hours at a time when their best work will be impossible because they are so tired. Women want increased flexibility in the curriculum, part-time and shared internships and residencies in all programs, 24-hour childcare at the hospitals and medical schools, and a general acceptance of the fact that many women and men are both parents and doctors — in training or in practice.

Many practitioners would like medicine to become less competitive and authoritative, more patient- than research-oriented, less fragmented into specialties, and more geared toward wellness than disease. Such an emphasis could be stressed in medical school

Table 3–3. Percentage of Professors in Medical Faculties (excluding Nursing) Who are Women at Eight Canadian Universities

University	Percentage of Professors Who are Women
University of Western Ontario	3
Queen's University	4
University of British Columbia	6
Université de Laval	10
University of Toronto	10
University of Ottawa	12
McGill University	14
McMaster University	15

— compiled from *Commonwealth Universities Yearbook,* 1985 and personal communications

Table 3–4. Enrolment of Women in Canadian Medical Schools, 1986–87

Medical School	Total Number of Students	Percentage of Students Who are Women
Université de Montréal	886	58
McMaster University	301	57
Université de Sherbrooke	401	57
Université de Laval	601	55
Memorial University	222	44
University of Ottawa	319	43
University of Calgary	217	43
University of British Columbia	496	41
Dalhousie University	394	39
University of Saskatchewan	300	37
Queen's University	296	36
University of Toronto	981	35
University of Western Ontario	419	35
University of Alberta	472	34
University of Manitoba	369	33
McGill University	627	33
Total	7301	43

— from Ryten, 1987

It is interesting to note that of those medical schools with greater than 50% women students, 75% are at French-speaking universities in Quebec.

39

by having classes or courses dealing with ethical issues such as poverty, abortion, euthanasia, reproductive technology, and financial issues; by admitting students who are not only brilliant academically, but who have a social conscience; by encouraging research by women on women's health and on hazards in the workplace such as anaesthetic gases and other volatile materials, infectious materials, and radiation and radioactive materials; and by hiring more women to teach in medical faculties and by placing those women in positions of greater power.

Medicine, like other university faculties, has more men than women on staff and pays the men more, but its treatment of women teachers is particularly bad. It is impossible to ascertain exact figures from Statistics Canada reports, which publish data for the "health professions and occupations," thereby grouping highly paid doctors with poorly paid nurses and physiotherapists. However, this category does list full-time full professors who are 7 per cent women, and full-time lecturers who are 64 per cent women (Statistics Canada, 1986b), which gives some idea of its hierarchy. In addition, the median salary of the men was $52 955 in 1984–85 and that of the women $38 464 (73 per cent), a discrepancy greater than in any other grouping, even engineering and applied sciences, where women faculty received 75 per cent of what men received (Statistics Canada, 1986b).

Chapter 4
Traditional "Feminine" Disciplines

To receive recognition as professionals, we have to be more scientific than the scientists.

A professor of nursing, 1987

There is a group of disciplines that has traditionally been thought of as belonging to women's sphere. It includes subjects that belong to the home (house science or home economics), that relate to personal and social health and nurturing (nursing, physical and occupational therapy, social work); and that concern teaching the young and reading (education, library science).

These disciplines gained status after the First World War as people began to look to the universities to supply experts for a variety of practical (as opposed to strictly scholastic) needs. Between 1920 and 1940, when the number of students at universities in Canada rose dramatically, the proportion of women students increased from 16 to 24 per cent. A large number of these women entered newly formed or newly expanded programs that were restricted to, or of especial interest to, women: education (156 in 1920 to 677 in 1940), household science (100 to 790), nursing (122 to 510), social work (85 to 146), library science (0 to 52), and physical and occupational therapy (0 to 121) (Harris, 1976, pp. 351–399). Women usually headed these new programs, and it was women students who enrolled in them.

During the rapid expansion of Canadian universities in the 1960s, many of these practical programs were shuffled aside because they were not academic enough. Some remained in the universities but were downgraded, while others moved to community colleges. In the financial cutbacks that have taken place more recently, these programs have been further downgraded, or, if men have been hired as professors to replace a number of the women, they may be able to hold their own because of this perceived "upgrading."

One example of an institute which has gone through a checkered history, as far as women are concerned, is Macdonald Institute in Guelph, which was affiliated with the Ontario Agricultural College (Ross, 1974). When this institute was founded in 1903, one of its three departments, Home Economics, was headed by a woman. The department and the institute grew steadily, even during the 1920s when the number of agricultural students slumped. Until 1939, the institute offered only one- and two-year courses to women, who were therefore less able to take part in campus activities than were the many male "Aggies" who took four-year courses.

In 1948, the institute was upgraded to the status of a college with a four-year program which offered a degree rather than a diploma. Dr. Margaret McCready was hired to be principal. The original departments of Nature Study and Manual Training were gone, and the three component departments were now Foods and Nutrition, Home Management, and Textiles, Clothing, and Design. These subjects continued almost always to be taught by women to a female student body.

In 1969, there was a drastic revision of the institute as it became a more integral part of the new University of Guelph under the direction of newly appointed Dean Janet Wardlaw. In keeping with its new higher status, more male faculty were hired. The three departments of the new College of Family and Consumer Studies were now headed not by three women, but by one woman and two men (Table 4–1). This trend of masculinization has continued for Consumer Studies and Family Studies whose faculties are now only 44 per cent (down from 67 per cent) and 68 per cent (down from 92 per cent) women. All the top administrators at the college are now men.

At the University of Windsor, the budget of the Department of Home Economics has regularly been slashed despite the fact that the program is very cost effective, has consistently high enrolments, and also has a good teaching record. Nor is the Home Economics Department duplicating work being done in other departments, as the administration claims; it studies some subjects that are not dealt with in other fields, and it approaches subjects from a different perspective than other disciplines.

It is becoming increasingly evident to members of the department (personal communication, February 7, 1987) that the standards for research (the ostensible reason for budget cuts) are not the main reason for the administration's lack of support. It appears that the administration is not interested in building up or changing the direction of the program to make it more successful — as has been the case with many U.S. home economics programs — because it does not in our opinion value the body of knowledge

Table 4–1. Gender of Faculty of the College of Family and Consumer Studies (founded in 1969) at the University of Guelph in 1971–72 and 1987

Department and School	1971–72 full-time	1987 full-time	1987 sessional
Dean of Faculty	woman	man	
Consumer Studies			
Chairperson	man	man	
Number of Men	5	9	
Number of Women	10	7	
Percentage of Women	67	44	
Family Studies			
Chairperson	woman	man	
Number of Men	1	11	2
Number of Women	12	23	14
Percentage of Women	92	68	88
School of Hotel and Food Administration			
Chairperson	man	man	
Number of Men	2	10	
Number of Women	0	4	
Percentage of Women	0	29	

— compiled from university calendars and interviews

on which the department is based. One sessional instructor was initially paid more for teaching a similar course in consumer studies when he taught it within the Faculty of Business Administration than within the Department of Home Economics. There is a (false) perception that scientific principles cannot be applied to this discipline, because it is thought of as merely an extension of housework. Contrary to that perception, several U.S. programs produce professional home economists, the scientific calibre and value of whose research is beyond question. Nevertheless, the home economics program at the University of Windsor faces a slow death over the next three or four years unless perceptions about its subject matter are changed enough to make increased funding feasible.

Nursing is another discipline known as a "female ghetto" because 96 per cent of nursing students are women. At the University of Victoria, faculty members of the School of Nursing have experienced the denigration of their field of study because it is thought to be unchallenging as subject matter (personal communication, February 7, 1987). They have also felt a need to become "more scientific than the scientists" so that their academic and professional value will be recognized. In addition, the nurturing aspect of nursing, a characteristic almost unique to this profession, has been derided as unintellectual. Nurses find themselves in a quandary whereby they must choose between being nurturing as their compassion requires, and being cold and calculating in order to project an acceptable "professional," "rational," image.

Alumnae of schools of nursing also experience a dichotomy between their theoretical status as professionals and their actual status in hospitals or community agencies where employers or doctors may treat them as menials.

Nursing students have for many years been portrayed stereotypically as "sexpots" (*Otherwise,* University of Toronto, November 25, 1986). In Nursing Orientation at the University of Toronto they have been portrayed as nubile young women in contrast to the macho men enrolled in engineering. Until very recently, orientation events involved such things as singing songs that praised the engineers for their maleness and indicated the nursing students' willingness to increase their bust size to win these men's acceptance. The women knelt down to the engineers when ordered by them to do so; they were tied to cannons and carried off by engineers; they participated in wet T-shirt contests, bedpan races, and slave auctions. In 1985, senior students began to revise the orientation, and it is planned in future to be fun without being degrading. The priority of the orientation should be to promote a group identity that the nursing students can be proud of, not to portray them as servile and stupid sex kittens.

Although library schools are willing to teach women to be librarians, universities are less willing to hire and promote them as professional librarians. About three-quarters of library students are women, but only two-thirds of librarians working at universities across Canada are women (Table 4–2). Fewer than one-third of library heads, who are responsible for the decisions and priorities of a university library, are women.

Despite the limited number of university library heads who are women, librarians are now facing problems related to affirmative action policies. At Carleton University, for example, the academic and staff employees' union ruled that if a woman and a man equal in qualifications were being considered for a position, the woman would be hired if there were a preponderance of men in the field, and vice versa. The librarians have now been informed that if a woman and a man with the same qualifications apply for a job in library work, the man must be hired because there are many more women than men librarians (personal communication, May 27, 1987). This could prove a devastating blow to a profession that, until now, has been more open than others to women. The few men who have become librarians in universities across Canada have been promoted more rapidly than the average woman, even if they seem to have the same or lesser ability. The discrimination for men in hiring may mean that they will soon dominate university libraries even more than they have in the past. Despite such dangers, many librarians remain unaware of political implications of hiring and promoting policies. One woman told us that there were too many women in her library and that more men should be hired to balance them. This egalitarian sentiment is noble, but strikingly absent among men in top positions at universities who usually do not notice a lack of women among their colleagues. If they do notice, they seem not to wish to rectify it.

Table 4–2. Percentage of Students of Library Science and of University Librarians Who are Women

	Full-time Total Number	Percentage Who are Women	Part-time Total Number	Percentage Who are Women
Students 1984–85:				
Undergraduate	161	66	317	74
Master's	720	76	306	78
Doctoral	18	78	5	20
University Librarians	367	67		
University Head Librarians	74	31		

— compiled from Statistics Canada, 1986 (Cat. 81-204), CAUT, 1986c, and Academic and Administrative Officers, 1985

When professors were poorly paid before the 1960s, there was little infiltration by men into the disciplines discussed here, which were seen as suitably feminine ones. When all university teachers began to be better paid in the 1960s and after, men began to enter even these disciplines, finding that by doing so they were seen as "upgrading" them. In return for this increased prestige of a discipline, women in it were less often hired and promoted. With affirmative action policies that will benefit men more than women, women can only expect further erosion of their former strongholds. As for librarians, one should applaud a more even distribution of women and men in every part of the university, yet when this more even distribution goes only one way, and when male-dominated areas continue to exclude women, it is difficult to do.

Women are well aware of their present vulnerable double-bind position in these feminine disciplines. If a discipline continues to have a large number of women professors, it is likely to be seen as an unimportant one which deserves little funding for teaching and research. If it is seen as worthy of increased funding, it is likely also to be hiring and promoting relatively more men compared to women. Universities see as axiomatic the correlation between prestige and male presence.

Chapter 5
Women's Studies

*One indication of the subordinate position of women in the
University is the extent to which academic concerns of
particular relevance to women are marginalized in the
curriculum and in the research priorities of the professorate.
Some departments in which women's concerns might well
occupy a major place offer no provisions for their study.*

Ad Hoc Committee on the Status of Women
A Future for Women at the University of Toronto, 1986

As we have documented in the preceding section, many subjects
are taught in a way that, at best, prevents widespread acceptance
of feminist ideals, and, at worst, reinforces traditional gender
stereotypes. Programs in women's studies are in many instances
the only way to compensate for this sexism because they provide
a more accurate view of the world.

Twenty-eight of Canada's universities offer some form of
women's studies program at the undergraduate level (Brodribb,
1987). Some universities offer either a minor, a diploma, or a cer-
tificate, while others offer programs that can be extended to form
a major or a double major. There are only two graduate programs.
Women's studies programs were first offered in the 1970s, while
Trent University inaugurated its program in 1987. Two universities have formal institutions to administer their programs: Concordia has the Simone de Beauvoir Institute, and Mount Saint
Vincent the Institute for the Study of Women (which publishes
Atlantis). Although the Simone de Beauvoir Institute is one of
the most renowned centres of women's studies in Canada, it did
not offer a full-time tenure track position until 1986 (Brodribb,
1987).

The programs themselves usually contain a few "core" com-
pulsory women's studies courses, and a group of related courses
of which a certain number must be completed to satisfy the stated
requirement. The total number of courses approved for women's
studies programs varies from a few to almost 50 at the University of Toronto. In 1985–86, 1845 students at the University of
Toronto took women's studies courses (personal communication,

June 16, 1987). But courses included in women's studies programs are not always mainly about women. At Wilfrid Laurier University, for example, Women's Studies Approved Courses (1987–88) include Psychological Anthropology; Greek and Roman Mythology; Evil and its Symbols; Religion and the Crisis of Daily Life; and Sociology of the Family. At the University of Toronto, women's studies courses include Studies in American Literature; Victorian Thought and Manners; Natural Science and Social Issues; Philosophy of the Emotions; Morality, Medicine, and the Law; Psychoanalytic Approaches to the Study of Social and Political Issues; Society and Interpersonal Relations; Sociology of Work and Occupations; and Socialization. Surely all of these courses are as much about men as women. Their inclusion seems to reflect a desire to provide as many courses as possible to be counted toward women's studies, and perhaps insufficient desire to support new courses.

Universities that offer women's studies programs do not give them a high priority. For example, at the University of Toronto, the popular Women and the Law course ordinarily attracts about 70 students a year, making it a lucrative "bread and butter" staple for New College, which organizes this program. The university was unwilling to supply enough teaching assistance to mark the papers from the course, however, so the professional lawyer who taught it was unable to give the course in 1986–87. It was cancelled, leaving many dozens of students disappointed (personal communication, June 16, 1987).

Women who specialize in women's studies often find that their hope for tenure is slim. Dr. Marylee Stephenson, a sociologist who was one of the leaders in the field of women's studies in Canada, lost her fight for tenure, and thus also her job as an assistant professor at McMaster University, in 1979 (*Globe and Mail,* July 4, 1980). She had developed new courses, and edited a textbook and a newsletter in women's studies that attracted graduate students from across the country, but her scholarship was judged inadequate by her department. Stephenson was praised for her teaching, which attracted 300 students a week to one course, but information she provided encouraged her students to be skeptical of what they were learning in other courses. A colleague said that McMaster "felt very threatened by her because her field involved women reflecting on their changing role. It was very threatening for an established institution." Seventy-six individuals or representatives of groups from across Canada sent letters of support and evidence of Stephenson's work to the McMaster Tenure Appeal Tribunal which studied her case. Although her teaching and service to the community were judged "clearly outstanding," she was still denied tenure (letter, September 4, 1979).

Since women are in the minority among professors, and feminist women in an even smaller category, it is perhaps not surprising that feminists are not always available to instruct women's studies courses. Even though this is understandable, it is a serious problem: non-feminists teaching women's studies courses can do more harm than good to students' already sexist perceptions of women. The accepted views on matters such as women and the law, or labor economics, are well known enough to appear correct and just unless a feminist perspective is given adequate consideration, an accomplishment that can be made very difficult for even the most confident feminist teachers (see Bezucha, 1985, p. 89). For instance a Philosophy and Women course at one Ontario university was transformed because an outspoken sexist male student challenged the feminist opinions of the instructor and the materials. The student pressured the instructor until she agreed to debate the "fairness" of sexual discrimination with a (male) professor who favored sex discrimination. Not only was this incident one that is unimaginable in traditional, male-stream courses or between a woman student and a male teacher, but time was wasted that should have been spent on the subject of the course, and a feminist perspective was debased before a class of largely non-feminist students. The course succeeded more in reinforcing stereotypical beliefs than in raising feminist consciousness.

Not only some students, but many faculty are opposed to feminism and women's studies on their campuses. One professor of geology at Queen's University wrote (in a letter which he claimed had wide support, especially in the Science Faculty):

> There can be little doubt in anybody's mind . . . that the course [in women's studies] is taught by feminists and is solely concerned with orthodox feminist ideology. We regard this as a blatant and entirely unacceptable attempt to politicize legitimate academic activity at Queen's and we wish to take this opportunity to exercise . . . influence in redressing an intolerable distortion of our academic system. (Toogood, 1987)

This brings us to the question of women's studies students: Who are they, and why do they take the courses? While the majority of students enrolled in the courses are women, a sizable number of these seem not to be feminists. Whether new ideas are presented and discussed depends on how the course is conducted, as the above example illustrates. Feminists in women's studies courses may find an opportunity to discuss and study material not treated in other courses, or they may find yet another example of sexism. Some men who take the courses may genuinely be interested in learning about women; if this is the case, it is a pity that some find the class atmosphere anti-male and withdraw. (Whether the atmosphere is genuinely anti-male, or whether men are so accustomed to being the centre of attention that they perceive a focus on women as being anti-male is another question, and a very important one.) Other male students have less noble motives; one man at the University of Waterloo stated flatly that he was sick of listening to feminists and had taken the course to get ammunition against them. It was probably men such as this who broke the Women's Studies sign and urinated on the program's door one Hallowe'en. Since males are still given preferential treatment in some courses, a man with an anti-feminist attitude who is allowed to dominate discussion can sidetrack or destroy a women's studies course which lacks equally strong feminists.

Women's studies programs are at present the best, if not the only, way to introduce a feminist perspective to university studies. Yet they are underfunded and susceptible to non-feminist infiltration. A few tenured professors regularly teach women's studies courses, but since there are no tenured professors of women's studies in Canada, the discipline could easily be wiped out at any time should university administrations decide to do so. University students continue to learn little about women unless they enrol in the women's studies courses, but they only enroll in these courses if they are interested in women to begin with. If sexist students and instructors are allowed to destroy the feminist environment of a women's studies course or program, feminists may find nothing better there than they do in other courses.

Despite the enormous need in Canadian universities for more properly taught women's studies courses and programs, some of those programs are being downgraded. (In the United States, 300 000 courses and 600 programs are offered [Holleran, 1985].) This may be in part because of financial restraints, which make faculties eager to retain as many students as possible within their own boundaries, to the detriment of interdisciplinary programs such as women's studies. Also, some believe that money spent on women's studies is wasted and should rather go to the long-established disciplines where, of course, women's concerns have for an equal length of time been ignored (Bercuson et al., 1984, pp. 150–155). The University of Manitoba cut its women's studies program budget for 1986–87 in half to $10 000 (*Herizons,* September, 1986). The co-ordinator of the program lost her job, and nearly half of the eighteen women's studies courses were eliminated, affecting 250 to 300 students. This reduction took place just at the time when the universities of Winnipeg and Manitoba jointly received an endowment from the Secretary of State for a Chair in Women's Studies designed for the development of this discipline. To receive this endowment, the University of Manitoba had committed itself to maintain the existing Women's Studies Program.

Integration of Knowledge about Women

Women's studies programs are only possible because of recent research carried out by women about women. Without this, there would be little women-centred information to impart to students. Even when there is a substantial body of knowledge that takes into account women's experience and perceptions, it may be difficult or impossible to have this included in general university courses. Yet unless such integration takes place, universities will not best serve women's and men's interests. Some feminists look to the day when all knowledge being discovered and taught at universities will have no gender bias so that women's studies will be redundant; other feminists are less sanguine about the effect feminism will have, and believe that women's studies will always be a necessary discipline. Most feminists are eager to have as much integration of research on women as possible into all university courses (see Franzosa and Mazza, 1984, and Schmitz, 1985).

If universities offered completely gender-neutral courses, each course in the arts would have to be completely restructured. It is not enough merely to add important women or research on women; the entire structure must be rethought so that men and their affairs are no longer the norm, with female subjects added. The content would have to be weighed carefully, and a feminist critique would have to be included to balance knowledge that comes to us from the past and is exclusively male-oriented. Each course would need a great deal of money and time to perfect. An extensive project of this nature which was instituted at Wheaton College and at other U.S. universities (see Spanier et al., 1984), is discussed in Chapter 11. No such effort has ever been mounted in Canada. Women who create new courses about women do so as thoroughly as time and resources allow, but teachers who have to cover a general course whose curriculum is already set have difficulty adding much content about women. Most professors handle new research on women by ignoring it in their courses. If women ask to have it included, they often are also ignored.

Women who have attempted to balance the male bias of course content have run into serious problems. When Sheila McIntyre (1987) tried to bring a woman's perspective to her law classes at Queen's many of her male students responded drastically. They could not prevent her from lecturing as she thought appropriate, but they could try to destroy her credibility. They depicted her and two other women professors pornographically on the walls of the men students' bathroom. The women were named and cartooned naked in a sexually repugnant manner or as having odd sexual propensities. McIntyre was portrayed as a lesbian and was said to suck "clits and tits." She writes: "You should try walking into a classroom feeling human when you know 60 per cent of the student population may have read such entries, may find them amusing or the ultimate insult, and the words stay on the wall." (p. 9). She noted that male professors were also insulted in the graffiti, but they were denigrated for their teaching ability or for their lack of intelligence, not for their sexuality. Only two men were so abused, one who was considered to be gay and the other the dean who lived with a feminist.

Chapter 6

Research

Because research on women is perceived as being outside of the mainstream, biased, political, unimportant, and/or inaccurate, women whose interests and work lie in this area are at an obvious disadvantage in being published. This may be especially true if they challenge time-honored male-centered traditions and assumptions.

Angela Simeone
Academic Women: Working Towards Equality, 1987

As we shall see in this chapter, some feminist research is being financed by the government and some is being carried out at universities, but there is little grant money available and few feminist faculty. Much of women's efforts to learn about women, therefore, has taken place outside the universities. Women across Canada are doing research by writing and reading books and articles, setting up feminist libraries of their own, organizing workshops, mounting displays of women's art, establishing medical and psychological self-help groups, making and watching feminist films, and talking about women's experiences (see Thompson, 1983).

This is a tremendously important development. If knowledge about women came only from the universities, it would be biased from a male perspective, and although individual women and their works might be studied, they would be viewed, if at all, in the context of male-centred disciplines. By having knowledge of women developed from women's experience at the grass roots, we are far more likely to gain important new insights into women's condition.

Nevertheless, many billions of dollars from women as well as men taxpayers go to support universities, and they should address the concerns of women as thoroughly as they address those of men. Women's activities such as those listed above will always take place outside of our universities; they should take place within them as well.

Despite the lack of research on women in the past, far more scholarly work is still being done on men and their concerns. The

Social Sciences and Humanities Research Council of Canada (SSHRCC, 1986) in 1985–86 funded 797 research projects with over $24 million, but only 8 per cent of these involved primarily individual women or women as a class. Nearly half of these projects (32) were funded under the Women and Work Strategic Grant program, so that only part of the money dispersed to women funded original research in which the researchers themselves decided what issues should be addressed.

The professors at universities across Canada who decide what research projects will be funded are nearly all men. In only 3 of the 34 selection committees for the 797 research grants and strategic grants were there more women than men (including the Women and Work Strategic Grant), in several there were equal numbers of women and men, but in most men predominated, once by as much as seven to zero. In votes about whether a feminist project should be funded, men nearly always made the decision.

Like the selection committees, the governing body of the SSHRCC (1986) is largely male. The Council consists of 15 men and 4 women (21 per cent), while the Advisory Academic Panel includes 9 men and only 3 women (25 per cent). The president, who represents the SSHRCC on nine other national or international academic bodies, is a man.

Male-oriented professors can promote men's work rather than women's not only by funding it, but in other ways too: in their writing of reference letters for their students for scholarships and grants; in inviting men, in preference to women, to give readings and lectures; in serving on Canada Council and other juries (which usually have more men than women) and recommending more men than women for individual grants; in helping to decide whether feminist periodicals and feminist research will be government funded; and in their recommendations about whose work the government should buy (and thereby endorse artistically as well as financially) or save for posterity in archival collections (Dagg, 1986, p. 40).

Because research at universities has been geared toward male concerns, we know far too little about things of interest to women. We know a great deal about war and politics, which have been men's affairs, but little about women's activities throughout history. We have ample research on individual men, but far less on individual women (which is not surprising since university and other archives collect the papers of far more men than women). Research on birth control has centred on hormonal modifications in women, rather than on a pill for men whose hormonal functioning is less complex. Until recently very little had been written about things that showed men in a woman-hating light — rape, incest, wife beating, and sexual harassment. Indeed "sexual harassment" only became an accepted term in 1974 (Kramarae and Treichler, 1985, p. 413).

It is impossible to tell whether women starting their careers receive less research funding than men with equal qualifications because all research proposals are different. However, in 1986 one woman who applied for a fellowship at the National Cancer Institute was asked if she planned to be married or to have children, which indicates sexist bias is still alive.

Research concerning women should be done from a woman's perspective, as Eichler and Lapointe emphasize in *On the Treatment of the Sexes in Research* (1985). For example:

- In literature, studies of the work of writers such as Sade, Mailer, and Miller, and of eroto-pornographic literature in general might seem to indicate new frontiers in female sexual liberation, whereas research from a female perspective may point rather to enslavement and new forms of women's oppression.

- For history, a woman's perspective might include such things as domestic life, the relations of the sexes, the rearing of children in different societies, and reproductive rights rather than on parliamentary politics, war, and commerce, activities in which men are centrally involved.

- For law, a woman's perspective would consider why women but not men have been restricted by certain laws and how the same law can affect women and men differently.

- In theology, women are often interested in the goddesses that predominated in early human cultures, and in sexist language and misogyny, which exclude women from full participation in many religions.

- In economics, researchers might consider why women can carry a double workload all their lives, yet have their labor unrecognized both socially and financially.

Special effort must be made to ensure that sexist concepts do not exist unnoticed in research projects. For example:

- A child whose parents work outside the home, often is said to be suffering from "maternal deprivation," never from "paternal deprivation."

- In the Western world agriculture is thought of as a male activity (which is not true even in Canada); when non-industrial societies are being discussed, the assumption is often made that farming is male work there too, even though it is almost always done by women. Thus women's contribution to the economy seems to be non-existent.

- In psychological tests, a question may be worded, "Do you think that women doctors are as good as men doctors?" This does not allow for a response. It also encourages the evaluation of talent on the basis of sex, which is an irrelevant factor that women are better doctors.

- Some professionals and researchers (as well as politicians) refer to wife-battering as "spouse abuse." This is a misleading term implying that husbands and wives are equally likely to be beaten, which is not true (Eichler and Lapointe, 1985).

Women who carry out research on their own are all too often unable to get their work published in a mainstream journal. Berta Losel-Wieland-Engelmann, for example, postulated that the extremely well-known German medieval epic, the *Nibelungenlied,* could have been written by a nun, rather than by a cleric or knight or minstrel. A female authorship would explain many of the enigmas that had puzzled academics for hundreds of years, including why the author knew little about hunting or war and sympathized with the women who were wronged in the story. Far from welcoming this new perspective, mainstream academics refused to publish Losel-Wieland-Engelmann's paper on the subject, or to allow a PhD student to address it. Losel-Wieland-Engelmann writes that academics

> probably do not cherish the idea that a poem which they always praised and venerated as a national monument could possibly be unveiled as nothing more than a well-disguised feminist manifesto which was intent on exposing men's injustice and meanness, stone-heartedness and greed, solidarity and conspiracies in their dealings with women. (1981, p. 90)

As a second example, although there are many studies in psychology on possible sex differences between women and men, it is difficult to get those that show no difference published in the literature. McDaniel writes, "Negative results, when the existing rubric is the search for differences, get file drawered. A 1979 study by Rosenthal which attempted to quantify the 'file drawer' on sex differences suggests that negative findings are much more common than positive ones, not surprising given the huge gender similarities which exist" (1987, p. 4).

Ironically, much sociological research has been carried out

because modern women, who often have a full-time position as well as sole responsibility for the family, have trouble managing both jobs at once (Spender, 1982, p. 141). Women working for money have been surveyed for their greater incidence of marital disturbance and breakdown, for the stress they have caused their marriages by having paid work, and for the problems their children face because of maternal (not paternal) deprivation.

The suppression of women's research occurs in biology as well as in the humanities and social sciences. Recently Anne Dagg wrote up some of the sexist ideas discussed in sociobiology in a scientific paper that she hoped would be read by animal behaviorists and sociobiologists. One of the points she made was that scientists have been changing data to make them fit sociobiological theories.

Science refused to publish her work although one reviewer wrote, "This article raises a number of issues that should be addressed in the pages of *Science*. Some are general such as the particular difficulties facing women in science, or the problem of updating ideas no longer held by specialists in a field but still alive in the general scientific community. Others are particular to behavioral biology, including the increasing use of words and concepts with specific human connotations to describe the behavior of nonhuman animals, or the general problem of subjectivity in behavioral observation" (letter, September 18, 1981).

The editor of *BioScience*, who also considered the paper, wrote, "I think that the issue you have raised is a most serious one," but refused to publish her work. One reason was that the referee did not agree with her objection to the use of anthropomorphic terms (letter, September 1, 1982).

Another referee wrote of a longer version of Dagg's ideas, "This is an interesting paper and I recommend that it be published in *Animal Behaviour*. This issue of the hidden agenda is an intriguing one that deserves more attention from scientists themselves, rather than remaining the province of sociologists, historians and the like, and I would hope that this paper will stimulate an extended discussion of sexual and other types of bias. In general the paper is well written and presented, although I have a few specific comments . . ." (letter, January 31, 1983).

Despite this reviewer's recommendation, the editor refused to publish it. He wrote, "I feel that you have selected your material in order to attack all ethologists. As one who is dedicated to the investigation of female choice in animals, I feel it is unfair that I should be lumped together with others who, no doubt, do take a sexist approach" (letter, January 31, 1983).

Journal of the History of the Behavioral Sciences also refused to publish the work, although the reviewers commented, "The author does us all a service by pointing out the heavy hand of male bias laid on by the male scientists of previous generations," and "The semantic problems do continue to plague that literature, as the author emphasizes in detail" (referee comments, June 20, 1983).

Although various university biologists who acted as referees expressed a desire to highlight sexism and sloppy reporting in science, these journals would not publish work that cast a shadow on predominating attitudes. Until major scientific journals are prepared to challenge mainstream behavioral biology, sexual bias in biology cannot be abolished. (Dagg's paper was finally published in 1984 in the *International Journal of Women's Studies*.)

All scholars would like to publish their work in the top journals of their discipline. If they publish in a small or little-known journal or in a feminist journal, their research will remain peripheral to their disciplines because many of these are not included in indexes such as the weekly *Current Contents: Social and Behavioral Sciences*, which lists as they appear the article titles of over 1300 journals. No Canadian journal about women is included among these selected journals, and we found only seven specifically about women from other countries.

Unless a new journal is accepted by such an abstracting service as runs *Current Contents*, it has little chance of becoming widely known and thus of having many individual or institutional subscribers. If a journal has an institutional affiliation, it can succeed because it is subsidized; if it has no such affiliation, it is likely to fail, as did the excellent *International Journal of Women's Studies*, published by Sherri Clarkson in Montreal. Because it was an independent journal, it existed entirely on subscription fees, which failed to cover its expenses. It began in 1978 and ceased publication in 1985.

A number of other factors militate against women's research. For example, it is more difficult for nurses than doctors to win funding, because the majority of men who award grants seem to take nurses less seriously than doctors. One male professor referred to "the girls" who taught nursing (personal communication, December 29, 1987).

As another example, researchers who publish more than others are more likely to receive further grants. The publishing record of a researcher is often taken as the total number of papers on which she or he is listed as author; even if ten people co-author a paper, each counts this paper as equal in value to one written by a single author. This works to the advantage of those doing research in fields in which co-authoring is extensive (as in medicine, science, and engineering) and to those who are involved in extensive networking in their disciplines. Both these categories include proportionately more men than women.

In addition, the few women who have done extensive research and then been accepted into administrative posts in the academic hierarchy may face more discrimination than men. One such woman found that some of her grant proposals had referees' comments indicating that a woman so high in administration would not be able to do much good research because of her other commitments (personal communication, June 16, 1987). None of her male colleagues in the same situation had received such comments from reviewers.

The direction many universities are currently taking will also work against women. The Ontario government annually gives scores of millions of dollars to new "Centres of Excellence" based in universities that combine academic with industrial research. These new centres are all in technological and scientific areas in which women have seldom been allowed to participate. Their ascendance will disadvantage women at universities even more than at present. Greater emphasis on graduate compared to undergraduate work, a strategy which the University of Toronto is contemplating, will also work against women, who are less likely than men to be graduate students.

The negative attitude toward feminist academics means that many women censor themselves. One anthropologist at a conference on gender at Wilfrid Laurier University in January, 1987, noted that she never had any trouble getting her books and articles on Native women published: "I make sure I never use flag words like "feminism' and 'patriarchy,' of course," she said. "That would turn everyone off right away."

"But how can you do a feminist analysis of your work, if you can't use such words?" another woman asked.

A man then broke in: "Of course you have no trouble getting published. If I were a publisher, stories about Indian women wouldn't bother me. But books that threaten me and other men, feminist books, no way."

There is also less psychological support for women than for men to carry out research. One professor at an Ontario university whose husband is also a professor finds that her friends are amazed that she will go away for months to do research on a sabbatical, leaving her husband behind. Yet men often go away for up to a year without their wives and children and no one comments about it. This double standard infuriates her, especially since she is more eager to do research than is her husband.

Chapter 7
Administrations, Professors, and Staff

Sexual discrimination is perhaps the most serious problem in higher education today. It is serious because it cuts out or it cuts down fifty per cent of the potential competition for university jobs and therefore lowers the quality of university teaching and research. In the name of excellence, women are effectively frozen out of higher education. In the name of excellence, it is excellence that suffers.

Joan Abramson, 1975
in Simeone,
Academic Women: Working Towards Equality, 1987

Administrations

The administration of a university is the force that guides it; it seems safe to say that, with the possible exception of Mount St. Vincent, which has a stated commitment to women, the administrations of all Canadian universities are largely uninterested in women's problems. Most universities have committees that address problems related to sex, but nowhere does there appear to be a strong desire to achieve equality for women and men. If there were, sexist attitudes and practices could be seriously combatted. Universities could take a small fraction of the billions of dollars they spend each year and rectify previous imbalances. They could hire large numbers of women presidents, vice-presidents, deans, and faculty, and they could award as many honorary degrees to women as to men.

In the fall of 1986, the executive heads of the 65 member institutions of the Association of Universities and Colleges of Canada (AUCC) passed a "Statement on the Status of Women in Canadian Universities." This statement read in part:

As educational institutions, universities have a special responsibility to play a formative and exemplary role in shaping a society that enables women to pursue, as freely as men can, careers appropriate to their talents and inclinations. Universities must ensure that the principle of equal treatment for both men and women informs all levels of institutional decision-making. (CAUT *Bulletin,* May, 1987)

These are stirring words, but the institutions involved have done almost nothing to implement them, as two subsequent surveys by the AUCC have shown (CAUT *Bulletin,* May 1987). One survey found that only 5 of the 65 member universities have formal policies on gender-neutral language, although other universities noted that they rely on informal practice to monitor university publications for gender-neutral language. Eight universities are thinking about gender-equal environment, for example through affirmative action clauses in union contracts. No university has a policy regarding gender-neutral curriculum. The study reported that some university administrators are concerned about how to implement such a policy, while others warn of "conflicts" which might emerge among students, professors, and administrators should such a policy be adopted.

In the second survey, the AUCC asked administrators of the 65 universities whether formal employment equity policies existed at their institutions. Of those that replied, 16 said no policy existed, 12 said they were studying the idea, and 13 reported policies in place. Most universities, therefore, are apparently not even considering equity policies, despite the grand statement about women they had approved.

Ontario universities' lack of interest in women was evident when these universities were reviewed in 1984. Three men were chosen for the Bovey Commission, but we can find no evidence that any university objected to the absence of women. The Commission's mandate was to "contribute to the intellectual, economic, social and cultural foundations of society," yet in its final report it ignored the concerns of women students and the need for more women professors. When Anne Dagg appeared before the Commission, two of the three commissioners asked questions that indicated they had no understanding of systemic discrimination. For example, chairperson Edmund Bovey said that there was no real discrimination in universities because women with talent, such as Lorna Marsden, had no trouble being hired and rising to the top of their institution. Nor did the commissioners pay attention to other women who noted: "The under-utilization of the talents of the educated female population, and the discrimination against women in universities, whether practiced consciously or unconsciously, is a national disgrace" (Symons and Page, 1984, p. 201).

Dagg wrote to the Toronto *Globe and Mail* pointing out the sexist bias of the Commission and its report, but her letter was not published, nor was any other on this subject; the dissent of a large group, dissatisfied with how public money is spent for higher education in Ontario, was allowed no voice. Other Canadian university women are no better off than are those in Ontario.

University committees formed to "deal" with women have few teeth. At the University of Waterloo, the President's Advisory Committee on Equal Rights for Women and Men (PACER) was set up in 1974 to ensure that women and men were treated equally at the university. It has been in operation for 13 years, but still this university has proportionately fewer women professors than any other in Canada. PACER is impeded in part by having to work in a strictly private and confidential way; if the president chooses to ignore its recommendations, publicity cannot be mounted to make him change his mind. A recent indication of its ineffectiveness is the discontinuance of the Dean of Women's position. It has been replaced by the position of Dean of Students. The new dean, a man, says, "Whatever was available to women should be available to men. We should be concerned with all students" (*Imprint*, January 23, 1987).

There is reason to doubt the president's commitment to women because of the yearly Kitchener-Waterloo Oktoberfest Beauty Pageant, which requires of the entrants virginity, never having had a live-in relationship, never having had an abortion, and being between the ages of 18 and 24. This event has been held for years each October on the University of Waterloo campus. Each year women protest at this sexist exhibition on campus and each year the administration books it again into the Humanities Theatre. In 1985, over 1500 students signed a petition opposing the pageant being held at the university. Many well-known people supported the opposition, including Marion Dewar, former Mayor of Ottawa, who wrote to the president, "Surely we do our young people, of both sexes, a grave disservice in continuing to promote the young, beautiful virgin as the ideal woman. As university president, you will be aware of the many studies which show the effect this stereotype has on society's expectations of women's capabilities and on interpersonal relationships" (*Imprint*, February 14, 1986). Despite such arguments the president again refused to ask that the pageant be held elsewhere in 1986 and 1987, claiming that "the University should not establish itself as a censor or moral judge." People who feel that such sexism undermines women's quality of education and their working environment can go to the Ethics Committee of the university, whose very existence indicates that the university believes there *should* be moral standards on campus. However, the Ethics Committee reports to the president, so there is little hope of change.

All universities have appeal procedures for academic problems, but these do not necessarily work in practice and may not address sexual discrimination. For example, many women students in architecture complain of discrimination against them (Iacobucci, 1984, p. 17). One architectural school in 1985 admitted about as many first year women students as men, but following the first term far more women than men were failed in studio, a basic subject. The faculty of studio classes are especially powerful, since criteria for judging student competence are subjective and easily manipulated to create exclusionary hurdles against women. A student who feels she is being discriminated against because of her sex is told to document her complaints in a letter to her advisor. Her comments then go to the teacher against whom she has complained, who is almost certain to disagree vigorously with her accusations, which likely address his ability and integrity. It is an exceptional (non-existent?) student who has the assertiveness and self-confidence to carry her concerns beyond this level of hierarchy.

Some universities are willing to pay lipservice to the concept of improving women's status, but refuse to make even the kinds of changes that would cost no money. For example, President George Connell of the University of Toronto wrote in the March/April 1985 issue of the University of Toronto *Graduate*: "We also owe it to ourselves and to the society we serve to monitor our continuing progress in the creation of an environment which gives women the best education we have to offer, and which freely gives them visibility for their achievements."

Taking the president at his word, Anne Dagg sent him material urging that the graduates of the University of Toronto no longer be called *alumni*, which refers only to men (as the plural of *alumnus*), but both *alumni* and *alumnae* (plural of *alumna*), which would include the many thousands of women who have graduated from this university. This is easily written as Alumni/ae. Such a change would seem to be not only accurate and polite, but also common sense, since the university often requests money from its graduates, and many women do not give money to causes that consider them men. President Connell never answered the letter, and shortly thereafter the neutral name of the graduates' magazine, *Graduate,* was changed to the sexist name University of Toronto *Alumni Magazine*.

While alumni (sic) magazines are not the direct product of university administrations, they certainly reflect the guiding philosophies of the universities that support them. The *Graduate* was no exception. In an article about a medical student we are told he "never consciously flaunts his intellectual machismo" in connection with his receiving a mark of 100 in first-year calculus (March/April, 1985, p. 22). Is intellect and/or mathematical ability somehow connected with being macho? An even more bizarre example occurs in an article in the same issue by George Ignatieff in which he relates what he did during the war as the private secretary to Vincent Massey. "I particularly remember a letter from a British housewife who explained that, because a Canadian soldier had spent his leave in her house, both she and her daughter were pregnant. To compound the felony, the visitor had taken off with her daughter's bicycle." Ignatieff then writes that he "welcomed these bits of comic relief in an otherwise exacting and exhausting job" (p. 14). Is Ignatieff's idea of comedy the probably unwanted pregnancies of two women in a time of war? If so, he is remarkably insensitive.

Professors

When universities were first founded sometime after 1100, students hired as professors those who could best teach them what they wanted to learn. Because professors at first lived wholly on the fees paid to them by students, the students maintained firm control. In fourteenth century Bologna, professors were fined if they missed a lecture or attracted fewer than five students to it. Professors who wanted to go out of town had to submit a deposit to the body of students to ensure their return (Haskins, 1984). One story indicates both that there were women faculty and sexist treatment very early in the history of universities. Novella of Bologna was said to be so beautiful that she had to wear a veil so that her appearance would not distract her students (Altman, 1980, p. 18).

The days are long past when students had any real say about which professors are employed at a university. Professors within each department now hire their colleagues, and they determine the characteristics required of applicants. Candidates must have acquired a great deal of knowledge in their field (usually by way of a PhD), be willing and able to carry on original research, and frequently have proved themselves to be good teachers. All too often they must also have connections in the "old boys" network, and be men.

Table 7–1. Percentage of Full-time University Teachers Who are Women for Selected Years 1921 to 1984–85

Year	Women as Percentage of Total
1921	15
1931	19
1941	17
1953	18
1960–61	11
1970–71	13
1980–81	16
1984–85	17

— compiled from Vickers and Adam, 1977 and Statistics Canada, 1986b

In the United States there is much consternation because only 28 per cent of all faculty positions are held by women. In Canada the number drops to 17 per cent. At the current rate of increase, it will take over one hundred years for women to gain full equality as professors. We know that women and men have equal intellectual abilities, and we know also that women's life experiences differ from men's. Yet women teachers have largely been excluded from our higher centres of learning. Thus, not only are universities being staffed by men of lesser ability than that possessed by the many women who have not been hired, these institutions represent and validate only a portion of human experience.

Many people rationalize that more women are being hired all the time, so that before long women and men will be equally represented among professors. This sounds hopeful, but the facts indicate otherwise (Table 7–1). The percentage of women teaching full-time in universities was higher in 1931 and 1953 than it is today, when there is so much rhetoric about needing more women. The percentage of women professors fell during the Depression because married women were either forced or persuaded to resign. It fell again during the period of expansion of universities in the late fifties and sixties because universities hired hundreds of men but few women. Universities were in a position to offer much higher salaries than they had in the past, and men, often from outside the country, were happy to accept them. The importance of money was illustrated when Waterloo Lutheran College gave up its religious affiliation and became Wilfrid Laurier University in 1973 so that it could obtain full provincial funding. One of the first things it did was fire four women from its faculty and

65

hire 64 men. The women, who were without tenure, had been willing to work for years at a low salary; when a high salary became possible, the university decided it no longer needed them.

Many people are aware that women have made some gains as professors since 1960; what is less well known is that there have also been losses. In agriculture and biological sciences and in education there are now fewer women teachers than there were in 1960–61; in fine and applied arts there are fewer than there were in 1970–71 (Table 7–2). In engineering and applied sciences, and in mathematics and physical sciences, women have made only small gains, whereas in the health professions and occupations women have made no real progress at all. Obviously it is naive to assume a trend that more and more women teachers will be hired, as will be discussed later in this chapter.

Table 7–2. Percentage of Full-time University Teachers Who are Women, by Field, Selected Years 1960–61 to 1984–85

	1960–1961	1970–1971	1980–1981	1984–1985
Education	28.7	20.1	23.9	25.8
Fine and applied arts	15.2	24.6	21.3	23.9
Humanities and related	10.7	16.9	18.6	19.6
Social sciences and related	8.3	9.3	14.1	15.9
Agriculture and biological sciences	19.0	15.9	16.2	16.7
Engineering and applied sciences	0.9	0.6	1.3	2.0
Health professions and occupations	23.4	20.9	23.4	23.8
Mathematics and physical sciences	3.9	4.4	4.6	5.3
Total	11.4	12.8	15.5	16.7

— compiled from Statistics Canada, 1986b

Although there are few women teachers in any discipline, some disciplines have even fewer than others (Table 7–2). In education, fine and applied arts, and the health professions and occupations, about one-quarter of full-time teachers are women, but in engineering and applied sciences, and in mathematics and physical sciences, five per cent or less of full-time teachers are women. This dearth is undoubtedly tied in with society's stereotype that women are not suitable for these subjects, but in addition the virulent women-hating displayed in engineering schools creates obstacles that keep women away from this discipline. Various studies have showed that women students do better if they have women role models to emulate, but such models are almost non-existent in engineering and physics. In addition, the near absence of women professors indicates to laypeople that higher education is really a man's world where women have little part. Canada loses a tremendous pool of human resources by discouraging women students from these non-traditional discplines.

Hiring

For decades it has been common for scholars to protest, at the observation that their department or university has few or no women professors, that this is because few or no women are trained for academic work. They claim that the university would hire women, indeed would *love* to hire women, if only women applied. If only *qualified* women applied. They blame women — too few have completed postdoctoral positions, too many opt for motherhood and the family, too few would be dedicated to research. The editor of the University of Toronto *Alumni* (sic) *Magazine* states categorically, "The fact is that, for many reasons, few women are attracted to academic life" (Winter, 1987, p. 4).

This is false reasoning. It completely ignores and invalidates any but the traditional male pattern of "study-then-career" to the exclusion of all else, a pattern that penalizes women, children, and men. What encouragement is there for women to pursue academic careers to the exclusion of all else when no one will hire such women? Society sanctions fathers who have successful careers and who may also be negligent or abusive parents. And if men who are scholars as well as fathers can be taken seriously, why should scholars who are mothers and who routinely work longer and harder than men, have their work discounted before they begin?

Although almost all professors extol the importance of merit (for example, women must *not* be hired preferentially to make up for past neglect because all hiring must be for merit), much hiring in the past has been not by merit, but by friendship and old boys' network. During the 1960s, when universities across Canada were expanding dramatically, the people hired were usually friends, or friends of friends. "We need someone in ethics," a philosopher might say, "I'll write to Joe who graduated from Columbia the year before me. He's sick of the Vietnam War and will be glad to come."

And come Joe did, often bringing in turn other colleagues and graduate students. Many departments and universities had nepotism rules that prevented women scholars from being hired along with their husbands, but some were so desperate for faculty that they hired wives in order to hire the husbands. Most of these women were granted tenure, as were their husbands, and both still staff Canadian universities, the men in their thousands, and the few women too. But this has proved to be a mixed blessing for these women no less than for their successors. Because these academics were not necessarily hired on merit, they are often not particularly productive, and because the women tend to hold fewer advanced degrees than do the men, they have been used both as examples of why more women should not be hired and as examples of how "generous" universities have been in hiring less qualified people who are women. These women, whose careers have been overshadowed by their husbands' and by circumstance, are now (as previously) unesteemed by their employers and students and may be blamed by younger, ambitious, and highly trained women for the part they play, however unwillingly, in maintaining universities' exclusionary policies. It is far easier to blame people than it is to recognize a vast and apparently unstoppable system.

At present, because few vacancies open up each year in universities, each available position becomes something infinitely precious; its filling is discussed and plotted by a department for many months. Everyone knows about the push to hire women, but when the competition is a male postdoctoral fellow in the "old boys' network," the quarrel over who shall win the coveted post may be bitter. All too often the man wins. It is men who almost always decide the winner, and it is men who strongly support the male scholar. The reasons for the choice are often amazing:

"He is one of us. He's brilliant," they will say, if questioned.

"He has a wife and child to support."

"He's bought a house in the area and has a large mortgage."

"He's an excellent squash player. He'll make a good fourth."

The woman who has no such cogent reasons for being hired is out of luck. No matter how brilliant she is, she is often told:

"Your work is excellent, but your research area is not quite what we're looking for."

"I agree you've taught many undergraduate courses, but the department needs someone with experience teaching graduates." (Or vice versa as the occasion demands.)

"We're looking for someone with a solid background of committee work."

"You've published dozens of papers, but not in the right journals, I'm afraid." (Only the department members know that the "right" journals, too, change conveniently with the occasion, and are the ones she hasn't published in.)

"We've decided not to fill the advertized position after all." Then they quietly give the job the following year to a male friend.

Because of the current crisis in funding, Canadian universities are increasing the number of term appointments for newly hired faculty and decreasing tenure-stream positions. Women are disproportionately represented in the short term positions, where a great deal of teaching is required and where they have little time for research (Ad Hoc Committee, 1986). Without the opportunity to research and publish, their chances of ever gaining a permanent foothold in academia are slight. Indeed, some departments do not bother to interview women in such jobs when a tenure-stream position becomes available, preferring instead to consider academics from other universities. More women have been hired recently than in the past, but present gains may prove illusory if these scholars have been hired in short-term positions without hope of gaining tenure and thus a permanent job. In addition, the number being hired is less, proportionately, than the number of newly graduated doctoral students who are women. In 1980, the federal government appointed 94 Natural Sciences and Engineering Research Council (NSERC) University Research Fellows (84 men and 10 women) to do research at Canadian universities. It was hoped that these people might in time become professors. Of this group, 80 per cent of the men but only 50 per cent of the women went on to obtain tenure-track appointments at Canadian universities (NSERC letter, October 20, 1986). The Council did not collect information on the gender of nominees for the NSERC awards after the first year, so no more data are available. It is interesting to note that, increasingly, universities and governments are providing data to the public that prevent analysis for sexist bias (Dagg, 1987).

In 1985, Ontario set up a Faculty Renewal Fund that provided the province's universities with money to cover a five-year period and provide 500 new teaching positions. At first, the fund had "some slight impact" in hiring more women and was beneficial in giving publicity to women's issues, but "little now remains besides some pious hopes." Naomi Black notes that although the fund was to be used in part as an affirmative action hiring tool for women, other of its goals militated against women. One of these goals is to hire young faculty (women are usually older than men when they apply for work because they have been slowed down by financial difficulties and family responsibilities); another is to hire faculty "consistent with the aims, objectives, and existing strengths of each institution." She writes:

> The "aims and objectives" of existing institutions have never included increase in the proportion of women in the faculty; their "strengths" and, even more, their future "aims and objectives" are likely to be in fields where women candidates for positions are still few (the more so in an era emphasizing science and technology). (1988, p. 16)

Indeed, the Ministry of Colleges and Universities explicitly funds "positions not persons," and in 1987 it approved for each university a long list of fundable positions identified by field.

The status of women at universities will only change significantly if feminists are hired who work actively for change. But as long as there are few feminist faculty, their situation is perilous, as the following example shows. Soon after the controversy surrounding Sheila McIntyre's courses in law given at Queen's University, a rumor spread through the faculty that there had been a change in hiring policy (1987, p. 9). The students held a protest meeting that 180 people attended. Although six members of the Women and the Law Caucus had met the evening before to decide what they should say in favor of hiring women, and especially feminists, they were too intimidated at the meeting to speak. Not one student had the courage to suggest without qualification that more women should be hired. No one at all endorsed the need for more feminists. Instead, one man insisted that if more women were hired, academic standards would fall. McIntyre had not taught most of the men (nor the one woman) who spoke against her. They did not know her credentials, nor did they know who else had been interviewed for her position or what the credentials of these people were.

After this meeting, four male students went to the Principal to complain about the "decline" of academic standards in the law faculty. None had been McIntyre's students, but they cited her lack of competency to illustrate the decline, even though she has three degrees and even though her own students were later to give her good course evaluations.

Much later, when McIntyre spoke with a male student leader about the hiring issue, he agreed that her academic freedom had been undermined, that she had been condemned by unsubstantiated rumors, and that she had been deprived of a right to a public hearing and to know her accusers. He said the hostility had been generated because she was a feminist, not because she was a woman; the other women teachers had not been attacked. He summed up the events by saying cheerily, "Well, no real harm was done" (p. 9).

Actually, great harm was done. Sheila McIntyre had been devastated. Women students had learned that it does not pay to stick up for women. And many male students must have felt the destructive power that comes with being able to smash something one does not like. Feminism had become an invitation to, or justification for, attack.

Law school will reinforce the inequality of women until more feminists are hired (p. 11). As long as there are only a few, they are easy targets for abuse, and can come to believe that their problems are personal rather than institutional. McIntyre and many others believe that hiring women who are feminists is a priority, and that they should be hired in twos and threes. Perhaps the only place in Canada where this has happened is the Ontario Institute for Studies in Education, where from a nucleus of feminists a strong feminist presence among faculty, researchers, support staff, and students has evolved. The chances of this happening elsewhere, however, and particularly in law schools, are slim. Even women who feel strongly that they have been refused work because of sexual discrimination have no recourse because their cases are considered too complex to be resolved by any human rights commission.

Tenure and Promotion

Once a woman has been hired in a tenure-stream position, as a professor rather than a lecturer or demonstrator, her academic life becomes in some ways even more perilous than it had been previously. Although statistics concerned with the awarding of tenure are not available, anecdotal evidence and the information in Table 7–3 indicate that not only do many fewer women than men gain it, they have more difficulty doing so even when in tenure-stream positions. Joan Geramita of the CAUT Academic Freedom and Tenure Committee notes that although only 17 per cent of the professoriat are women, 40 per cent of the cases that come before the committee are from women (CAUT *Bulletin*, December, 1987).

The denial of tenure has the disastrous effect of terminating the woman's job as a professor, and usually ending her career at the same time, as few universities hire academics who have been

Table 7-3. Percentage of Full-time University Teachers Who are Women by Rank and Field, 1984-85 (excluding Quebec)

	Full Professors	Associate Professors	Assistant Professors	Lecturers	Total	Full-time Doctoral Enrolment 1984-85
Education	10.9	21.8	39.0	49.3	24.6	50.6
Fine and Applied Arts	8.4	16.9	30.4	47.9	21.7	43.1
Humanities and related	8.7	18.3	31.8	49.3	20.1	44.1
Social sciences and related	4.8	13.4	25.4	39.7	15.8	41.9
Agricultural and biological sciences	6.5	17.0	27.1	52.5	17.1	30.3
Engineering and applied sciences	0.4	1.2	3.7	9.5	1.6	7.2
Health professions and occupations	7.1	19.3	36.6	64.1	24.6	36.0
Mathematics and physical sciences	1.2	4.5	11.7	23.5	5.7	15.2
Total	5.3	14.9	28.1	45.5	16.8	32.6

— compiled from Statistics Canada, 1986a,b

found wanting at another university. The period between gaining a tenure-stream job and winning tenure virtually renders scholars inactive politically. A feminist who works openly for women before her tenure hearing courts disaster — people on her tenure committee may easily hold such work against her. Indeed, she may have to prove to them that she is *not* too women-oriented if she wants to keep her job. Tenure, in theory, was set up so that professors could speak as they wished without danger of losing their livelihood. Currently, its presence tends to jeopardize the career of young scholars who are committed to any but mainstream, conservative ideals. As one woman explained, "Every time I do some administrative work for the women's programs, my tenure prospects suffer. I have less time for mainstream research, and my colleagues hold my efforts for women against me" (personal communication, July 9, 1987).

The women who have been hired by Canadian universities have, on average, been kept at a lower rank than comparable men. Table 7–3 indicates that women have a far more difficult task than men in winning promotion in every subject area. Without exception, the percentages of women increase dramatically as one descends from full professor to associate professor to assistant professor to lecturer. How can universities possibly justify hiring women for 64 per cent of the lecturer positions in the health professions and occupations, yet restrict the number of women full professors in this area to 7 per cent?

To be promoted from one rank to the next, all professors and their work must be assessed by a departmental committee. Since the professors are far more often men than women, their male bias ensures that fewer women than men on average are promoted. The results are illustrated in Table 7–3. For this reason many women believe that rank at universities should be abolished. They feel that it is of no use, except to make those who have achieved promotions feel superior. Without the need to vault from one rank to the next to get ahead, professors could simply work away on their own, receiving merit pay if their work was good and none if it was not. Granted, men would still probably earn more money, since the awarding of merit pay would be subject to the sexual discrimination practised during promotion assessments, but the wage discrepancy between women and men would be less.

Salaries

Women are routinely at a salary disadvantage compared to men because they are promoted more slowly. Sexual discrimination appears, too, when salaries of women and men within one rank in a particular field are compared (Statistics Canada, 1986b, Table 6d). Full-time university women teachers in the "hard" sciences and health professions earn less than four-fifths of what men earn; they earn slightly more than four-fifths of men's salaries in the fields where there are traditionally more women (Table 7–4). When salary increases are negotiated each year, they are always given as a percentage increase which widens the gap between those earning the highest salaries (almost entirely men) and those earning less (proportionately more women). Five per cent of $60 000, for example, is $3000, while five per cent of $30 000 is only $1500.

Table 7–4. Median Salaries of Full-time University Teachers by Field and Sex (excluding Quebec), 1984–85

Field	Men's Salaries	Women's Salaries	Women's Salaries as Percentage of Men's
Education	49 144	40 686	82.8
Fine and applied arts	43 056	35 691	82.9
Humanities and related	46 966	39 568	84.2
Social sciences and related	47 292	37 971	80.3
Agricultural and biological sciences	49 408	39 339	79.6
Engineering and applied sciences	52 069	39 168	75.2
Health professions and occupations	52 955	38 464	72.6
Mathematics and physical sciences	49 140	39 216	79.8

— compiled from Statistics Canada, 1986b

Part-time Teachers

So far we have discussed full-time teachers. If we look at part-time teachers, we find proportionately many more women employed. Part-time workers in universities, as in most work, have notoriously poor working conditions. They are an administrator's dream:

- They work on a piece-work basis for far less than a full-time professor is paid: for three courses a part-time teacher may receive $9000 while a full professor earns $70 000 for three courses, committee work, and research.

- They often do superior work because they have more time to devote to it.
- They may relieve tenured faculty of tedious, large first-year classes.
- They can be easily dismissed if student enrolment is down.
- They usually aren't allowed sabbaticals, time off for research, laboratory space, or benefits.
- They can easily be fired and someone else hired if they ask for better conditions.

Part-time teachers seldom have bargaining power because they are short-term usually, and are seldom members of their university's faculty association. Many faculty association members see them as a threat to full-time jobs; they would like not to improve their status, but to reduce their number.

The picture is even more gloomy than this. Part-time work is usually badly paid unless it is done by professors working on reduced load. These teachers, who are usually men, receive very good salaries because their pay is prorated. In addition, they receive many, if not all, benefits, which are usually denied to part-time workers. If the part-time worker is a physician, lawyer, or other well-paid professional who lectures at a university, the lack of benefits is not a problem because his (or, rarely, her) main employment income is elsewhere. Women often have no other work, so the lack of a pension/benefit plan may be disastrous. A recent study of part-time workers at the University of Waterloo (Professional Women's Association, 1986) indicated that 83 per cent of part-time male workers had other jobs whereas only 54 per cent of part-time female workers had other jobs. The second jobs of two-thirds of the men were fairly lucrative professional practices or private consultancies. Only one-fifth of the women held such positions.

Benefits

Not only are women teachers' salaries on average less than those of men, but their chance of earning benefits along with their wages is much lower. As Table 7–5 makes evident, full-time faculty receive far more benefits than the part-time and short-term faculty. Yet those in the part-time and short-term teaching categories have far more need of benefits because their salaries are so small. The move from left to right in Table 7–5 is the move from more to less. Short-term teachers have equality with professors only in the use of athletic facilities, and even this is sometimes subsidized for the full-time professors. Maternity leave has only recently been obtained at many universities. The opposition from men has been strong, with comments such as, "The women will be pregnant all the time and who will do their work?" and, "Surely women won't want to be singled out because they are pregnant."

Staff

Universities, like governments and private companies in Canada, exhibit extreme stereotyping in their hiring practices. As we have seen, the well-paid positions such as professor and top administrator almost invariably go to men. The poorly paid jobs such as instructor, typist, and secretary go to women. A 1985–86 survey of Ontario universities showed that although 57 per cent of full-time non-academic positions were held by women, only 10 per cent of employees in upper-management and 33 per cent of those in middle-management positions were women. An analysis of the middle-management group demonstrated that 59 per cent of the men compared with 24 per cent of the women received salaries of $33 000 or more (*Council of Ontario Universities Committee News,* May, 1987).

Secretaries usually have the least favorable working space in any department. They are often relegated to uncomfortable and unpleasant windowless areas while managers and professors, most of whom are men, may (because of cross-appointments) occupy two or three attractive offices (Ad Hoc Committee, 1986, p. 17). Sometimes several women work in a single area where they have no private space and no personal privacy. It is inefficient and annoying to be expected to do detailed work while someone nearby is talking to a colleague, and it is impossible for someone who is always available to interruptions from any passerby to work efficiently. When technological changes are made in an office, the women staff are frequently neither consulted nor considered. There are few opportunities at present for promotion for secretaries, and little chance that their ideas or suggestions will be implemented.

Once a top administrator is hired, he is likely to be around forever. By contrast, low-paid secretaries at many universities have a difficult time landing a permanent job. Many women have

Table 7-5. Usual Benefits Coverage for Faculty in Universities of Atlantic and Western Provinces, 1985–86

	Status			
	Tenured Faculty	Non-tenured Faculty	Part-time	Short-term
Hospital & Medical Insurance	yes	yes	some	no
Extended Health Care	yes	yes	some	no
Long Term Disability	yes	yes	some	no
Life Insurance	yes	yes	no	no
Dental Plan	yes	yes	no	no
Sick Leave	yes	yes	some	some
Sabbatical Leave	yes	rare	no	no
Professional Development Allowance	yes	yes	no	no
Summer Stipends	"all ranks"	often	no	no
Overload Stipends	"all ranks"	often	no	no
Tuition Policies	yes	yes	no	no
Maternity Leave	yes	yes	?	no
Paternity Leave	very rare	very rare	no	no
Adoption Leave	rare	rare	no	no
Moving Expense Policies	yes	yes	no	no
Mortgage Loan Policies	rare	rare	no	no
Post-retirement Benefits	some	no	no	no
Mid-career Options	yes	no	no	no
Pension Plans	yes	yes	no	no
Day Care Facilities	yes	yes	sometimes	no
Athletic Facilities	usually open if available - see Chapter 8			
	presumably open if available			

— compiled from CAUT, 1986b.

worked full-time for years at universities as secretaries and administrators yet are considered, because of policy, as temporary term employees whose jobs can easily be terminated.

The despicable way in which women staff may be treated is illustrated in the case of Mary Warner, secretary of the History Department of Brock University from 1971 to 1986 (Harrison, 1987). Warner was asked by the Sexual Harassment Committee of the university to give information about a history faculty member who had been accused of unsuitable conduct by student and faculty members. Because she was a member of no association or union, she asked the president of the university, Alan Earp, if she would be protected if she gave evidence to the committee about what she knew to be a serious problem. Earp assured her she would, so she went ahead. Her appearance before the committee, however, did not remain confidential. After an excellent work record of fifteen years, things began to go wrong in her department. She was chastised for minute misdemeanors — being one minute late from lunch, or making a typing error. She was demoted to the typing pool, later given a temporary job in another department, and finally fired. In the succeeding nine months she was unable to find any other secretarial jobs in the Niagara Region where she lives. She has launched a $1.5 million lawsuit which is before the courts.

While Warner was being persecuted for appearing before the Sexual Harassment Committee, the man against whom the complaints had been brought had been told to resign if he did not wish to face an inquiry which would be launched because of the accumulated wealth of evidence against him. He did resign after receiving a better-paying offer from an American university. The contrast between the fates of the two protagonists is horrendous, as Deborah Harrison points out in her article. The male professor who practised sexual harassment of students now has a better job, while the female clerical worker who testified against him has no job, and may never get another. Women students undoubtedly also fared badly, or they would not have complained in the first place. Some have felt unable to take courses from certain faculty members. To assume that the formation of a committee to deal with sexual harassment and other problems affecting women will solve these problems is obviously silly.

Because secretaries are often called "girls" and treated like children, they sometimes act like children. At the main office in a service area at one university, a sign was posted on the wall, which said:

In this area sexual harassment
will not be reported
but it will be graded

The women employees working for low wages nearby seemed to find this amusing. This same sign was also displayed in other areas and in the office of an employment counsellor, who advised one student to remove any mention of feminism from her resume to make it more compelling.

Forms of address, too, are problematic. Secretaries in academic departments are almost always called by their first names by professors. They in turn often address male faculty by their title as Dr, or Professor. When secretaries address women professors by their first names and continue to address male professors with honorific titles, conflict increases between those workers within departments who most need to build alliances. Again, the men win, the women lose.

Women who are manual workers also fare worse in the workplace than their male colleagues. The custodial staff has both men and women who clean, but the men almost always earn more than the women. The University of Waterloo student newspaper, the *Imprint*, reports that the staff is well aware of discrimination in the work force. One custodian filed a complaint with the Ontario Human Rights Commission because she was told by her supervisor that she should not apply for a higher-paying custodial job — if she did, "all the women would try to apply." Women are usually paid $8.20 per hour for a second level (C2) job, while men are paid $10 an hour for a first level (C1) job. The woman, who had been passed over twice for the higher paying job, is quoted as saying, "I have eight years seniority. How come they promote people who have been here for only a few months when I have an excellent work record? I'll tell you. It's because I'm a woman, and they don't want to give the women who work at the custodian jobs the C1 jobs. It's considered the men's job." Subsequent to her complaint and appeal to the Human Rights Commission, she was promoted, and has since dropped the appeal (January 23, 1987).

Other female custodians agree with this woman, but they are afraid to take any action. One said,

> If they find out you've been complaining, they have ways of getting back at you. Everybody's scared. It's not just me. They can move you to a different floor every night if they want to or put you on a really hard floor for punishment. I'll tell you it's not fair and it's not right, but please don't use my name. (*Imprint,* January 23, 1987)

One woman who did finally succeed in moving from a C2 to a C1 category feels that she is being punished for her persistence, because she was moved from an arts building, where cleaning is easy, to an engineering building with high traffic areas where dirt is tracked in each day.

> "They're trying to break me," she says. "They're hoping it will do me in and then they'll say to me 'See? A woman can't handle this job,' but I'm going to stick it out. There are men who haven't been able to handle this floor and they know that. Sometimes I think I should just give up and go back to being a C2, but I fought for this. I'm a single mother and I can really use the money. You know I think that if they'd just treat us like human beings it would solve a lot of problems, but they don't." (*Imprint*, January 23, 1987)

The CAUT *Bulletin* gives another example of systemic discrimination at an Ontario university. The starting rate for a Clerk-Typist 3 is $8.72 per hour and for a Groundskeeper 2, $10.37 per hour. The Clerk-Typist must have a grade 12 education, 2 to 4 years of experience, be able to type accurately, word-process, answer enquiries, and have good office skills (December, 1986). Clerk-typists are women. The groundskeeper, who is paid more, needs a Grade 10 education, experience in grounds maintenance, good physical health, and a class D driver's licence. Almost all groundskeepers are men. That discrimination in the selection process for these jobs is deeply entrenched is evident at a student residence at the University of Waterloo: the groundskeepers are known as "greenmen," and the residence cleaning staff as "housemothers." The Federal Contractors Program (1986) and pay equity legislation for Manitoba, Quebec, and Ontario will probably not affect teachers in universities, but may help staff women who are presently ghettoized in low-paid occupations (CAUT *Bulletin*, June, 1987; *University Affairs,* March, 1987; Howell and Harris, 1987).

The permanent staff who oversee cafeterias and serve out the food seem always to be women, as do those who work as clerks in bookstores or as cashiers in gift and food shops. All of these jobs are poorly paid, rigidly supervised, and regimented. By contrast, the men who run universities have expense account lunches, take time off when they feel like it, and are out of the office when the spirit moves them.

Chapter 8

University Services

[The gap between men's and women's athletics] is apparent in insidious ways: The band which shows up at three-quarter time in the women's 'prelim' game; the athletic department's hype of the ice hockey game which does not extend to the field hockey game close by; the News Release wherein men's athletic achievements take up pages 1 and 2 while women's achievements may be found regularly on page 3; the athletic therapy room which is accessible only through the Men's Locker Room. . . .

Marilyn Pomfret
Toward Equivalence of Opportunity, 1986

Women's Centres

We have argued that a women's studies program is necessary if feminist viewpoints are to be solidly established on an individual university campus. Even with such a program, feminist ideas will not reach most students, since few of them take women's studies courses. A more populist method is to have a women's centre that acts as a focus for feminist resources and activities. Though a university women's centre may work closely with a women's studies program, the two may serve very different needs. The women's centre can be the place where the theory of women's studies is practised. The centre can educate mainstream students about gender inequality issues in a nonthreatening way, while the department of women's studies carries on more scholarly work. These two levels of educational activities are needed to reach as large a student population as possible. A university women's centre can also provide a link between feminist activities on campus and those of the larger community. The needs of both communities can be better served by having access to each other's resources. Contacts with feminists from outside the university can enrich the experience of feminist students and faculty.

Apart from serving a mainstream educative function, a university women's centre is necessary for the health and growth of feminist groups. At the very least, it provides workspace. Some activities, such as maintaining a resource centre or library, or producing educational events, cannot be carried out successfully without a centre. But the most important need a women's centre fills for feminist groups is a locus for the validation of feminist views. The rooms budgeted for the women's centre may be the only place on some campuses where a woman's perspective and experiences are valued. A women's centre affirms women's importance, and gives at least some space that women can call their own. Many men resent this, as did those at Carleton who broke down the door of the women's centre and trashed its literature and large display racks.

If provided with enough resources, a university women's centre can initiate innovative projects that benefit the entire university community. Vocational counselling tailored to the needs of women, assistance specifically for women returning to school, and a feminist legal aid service could fill gaps left by traditional services. Feminist counselling on personal matters as well as for rape, battering, sexual harassment, and sexist treatment could be provided, as could space for the development of women's culture through music, radio and television programs, plays, and creative writing. In all these areas, women need to have a safe place to discover what can be produced to counteract the general sexism that exists elsewhere on campus. These services are not special treatment for women; they are ways to provide women with what they need, in the same way that universities provide for men's needs.

A distinction must be made between places for women run by women students (women's centres), and those run by the administration of universities, which are not comparable. At the University of British Columbia there is an Office for Women Students, formerly the Dean of Women's Office, which has served women since 1921. It has five professional counsellors, a small resource library, and a welcoming atmosphere, but because it is entirely financed and run by the university, it does not initiate or support ideas that are unacceptable to the administration. There is no student-run women's centre at UBC, and thus no place for radical disagreement with what the administration is doing.

Because of years of persistent lobbying, some Canadian universities have opened women's centres; York University in 1975 and Carleton University in 1976 were among the first. The present 28 university women's centres (Canadian Federation of Students, 1986) are usually plagued with little or no funding and insufficient space. The centre at the University of Guelph is tiny, but it is funded through voluntary contributions (50 cents each) from all students. Centres are staffed largely or entirely by volunteers who work on such issues as sexual harassment, sexual assault, and birth control information. Other educational events include speakers, movies, pamphlets, Take Back the Night marches, and International Women's Day celebrations.

One of the longest campaigns for a women's centre has taken place at the University of Toronto. Planning began there in 1919, when $125 000 was donated so that women could have facilities for sports and meetings similar to those available to men in the men-only Hart House (which finally opened its doors to women in 1972). Over the years various plans for the centre were drawn up, but it did not materialize until 1986. When Dagg visited it on the day of its first birthday celebration in January 1987, she had difficulty finding it because someone had stolen its sign. However, with perseverance, she finally located it in the parlour of an old house. The room was fairly large, so that if one divides its area by the number of students it serves (30 000) at the University of Toronto, there would be at least several square centimetres for each woman enrolled at the university.

This Women's Centre did amazing things in its first year of operation. There were 3500 calls and visits. During the fall term of 1986, it hosted two gatherings, sponsored two conferences, and organized evenings of poetry reading, of films on Canadian women writers, and of a discussion of women and sport. It has lobbied for and/or supported the Ontario Task Force on Midwifery, the Teaching Assistants' Union, a campus policy on sexual harassment, improved summer jobs, and the inclusion of sexual orientation in the Ontario Human Rights Code. It produced a monthly newsletter, worked on babysitting problems of students who are parents, and arranged to take over the Women's Information Line, a city-wide information and referral service (Baxter, 1987).

All this effort cost money, and although many individuals and groups have supported the Centre to the best of their ability, it needed more money in the fall of 1986 to make up its $16 000 basic budget for 1987. It approached the University of Toronto Students' Administrative Council for general expenses of $5000, which is one per cent of its budget, then $3000, and then $2000. One member of the Council said, "The Lady Godiva Band gets $600 and does more for this campus than a Women's Centre" (*The Varsity*, September, 1986). All these sums were voted down, despite what the Centre has accomplished for students. Objections included the fact that the Centre is too pro-choice on the abortion issue, that it may duplicate some services that the university already offers (although the SAC itself constantly refers people to the Centre, presumably because of a lack of alternatives), and that by having a women-run collective it discriminates against men. The Administration of the University of Toronto has also refused to fund the Centre, although its budget is more than ten thousand times that of the Centre.

Women's centres were a feature often of the 1970s. Now that the conservative '80s are here, some women's centres are losing their funding. The Ryerson Women's Centre, that had been active for years, was recently closed altogether, ostensibly because of its "radical activities." The Women's Centre at the University of Calgary has also closed. At the University of Waterloo, a move that promised larger quarters resulted in the trade of a room that seated ten people comfortably (for a population of 15 000 students) to one that squeezes seven people.

No matter how small, however, a women's centre can act as a front line defence for women. For example, the student association at Carleton University banned a sexist poster from the Unicentre on advice from the Women's Centre there (*Charlatan,* September 11, 1986). As another example, when Mathematics and Engineering Societies "Spirit Pubs" were held in the winter of 1987 at the University of Waterloo, the bar menu did not include a requested drink called an "Athletic Supporter" because the pub manager felt that this name would get her in trouble with the UW Women's Centre (*Iron Warrior,* March, 1987).

Childcare

Women still carry most of the responsibility for children, so the availability of childcare facilities on campus is an important factor in the lives of many female students, faculty, and staff. Access to childcare facilities is linked to the opportunities extended to women, since their lack often impedes a woman's work outside the home. Many women teachers who do not have childcare facilities become mired in part-time jobs and low rank, are forced to resign, or avoid an academic career entirely. Of all the professions, that of university teaching is the one in which women have the least number of children; this is unsatisfactory if women professors are to be able to live as full a life as anyone else (CAUT *Bulletin,* November, 1986).

For many students, the absence of childcare facilities is a limiting factor in their full participation "in both the formal (classroom, laboratory, computer and library time) and informal (peer and faculty social activities, informal discussion, attendance at special lectures, workshops, extra-curricular activities) dimensions of their education." The demand for childcare on the part of women students has increased since the early 1970s as the number of women students, and especially part-time mature students, has increased. Today nearly one quarter of full-time students are mature students, many of whom have childcare responsibilities. Furthermore, a lack of childcare facilities is a factor in the decreasing enrolment of women as degree levels increase (CAUT, 1986a, pp. 9–18). As academic pressures mount, graduate students who are parents may find it essential to have access to childcare facilities in order to complete both the formal and informal parts of their studies.

Faculty members who are mothers also require childcare facilities. These women often face greater academic pressure than their male counterparts because of the demand that they represent women in research, teaching, and committee work. In addition, young female academics are often in their childbearing years during the period of eligibility for tenure. Even when a woman has tenure, professional demands of an academic career necessitate the provision of childcare.

The odd hours not only of students but of many university staff members (some faculty, many librarians, food workers, and cleaners) require special infant and childcare services. Childcare needs to be flexible, allowing for classes, meetings, and conferences that take place in the late afternoon, the evening, or on weekends. Students and faculty also need drop-in care for short periods of time, such as when the parent needs to use the library.

Although the need for childcare facilities exists at all universities, a study prepared by the CAUT reports that only 34 of Canada's 66 universities had day care centres in 1983–84 (CAUT 1986a, p. 6). Only eight provided infant care. Although the number of children requiring on-campus care is not known, the CAUT brief points out that the many women who bring infants to class shows that childcare provisions are inadequate. Most of the childcare centres in the CAUT study are funded exclusively by parent fees, although some received provincial grants; if it is inadequately subsidized, many students and staff cannot afford available childcare (Ad Hoc Committee, 1986, p. 5). Although at some facilities students and staff are given priority, there can be long waiting lists: the University of Calgary has a 400-name list waiting for 65 places, and the waiting period can be up to two years (CAUT, 1986a, p. 7); the University of Waterloo is preparing space for 15 infants in day care, but there is a waiting list of 70 infants. Usually there are no after-school, evening, or drop-in services, so that the activities of many parents are restricted.

More affordable and flexible childcare facilities are needed if women are to have equal opportunities for success in universities. The problem will not be remedied until "complementary systems of childcare and parental leave that are as comprehensive, accessible and competent as our systems of health care and education" are developed (Task Force on Childcare, quoted in CAUT, 1986a, p. 20).

Birth Control

Other university services that seem to treat women and men equally, often do not. A recent referendum at Wilfrid Laurier University over the issue of including birth control pills in the student health insurance plan reveals such a discrepancy in the provision of health care. The student body voted against including the pill by 63 per cent, after a previous referendum had passed the motion with a majority of 52 per cent. The main argument against including birth control pills in the health care plan was that birth control is a personal, and not a social, responsibility. Yet other drugs are supplied on a personal rather than a social basis, such as antibiotics for some illnesses and anticonvulsant medication for epileptics. The decision hurts women more than men because women are left with the responsibility for contraception more often than men are, and women suffer the consequences of unwanted pregnancy if contraceptives are unaffordable. Further, some women are prescribed birth control pills as a treatment for conditions such as pre-menstrual syndrome or pelvic inflammatory disease. In contrast to the sentiment at Wilfrid Laurier University, its near neighbor, the University of Waterloo, has acknowledged the need for birth control services by including contraceptive pills in its health care plan for several years, and by operating a birth control information centre funded by the students' association.

Recreation

Many Canadian universities provide games rooms (theoretically) for both women and men. Generally only men use these facilities, however, and their attitudes and behaviors create an environment that intimidates all but the boldest women. At

Carleton University, the central games area at the Unicentre has a large number of pool tables and pinball machines that are played almost exclusively by men. When women walk by, those men who are not "shooting" stare at them; though they may not intend to intimidate, women do not feel welcome there.

Sports

Outside classtime, women students interested in playing a competitive sport, or simply in getting exercise in an enjoyable way, sometimes have less chance than men to participate in university athletics. Women *are* interested in participating in athletic programs, as the report *Can I Play?* (1984), of the Ontario Task Force on Equal Opportunity in Athletics (OTFEOA), noted in its findings for Ontario universities. Its data are based on questionnaire replies from 12 of the 16 Ontario universities, but statistics from other Canadian universities indicate that the conclusions almost certainly apply across the country. This report reveals that in Ontario, more women than men were enrolled in degree physical education programs — of 2701 students, 58 per cent were women. Women are also far more interested than men in instructional programs such as aerobics, fitness, and aquatics when these are provided. At Carleton and Queen's, 79 per cent of the 5804 students in such programs were women.

Despite this high level of interest among women, both intramural and intercollegiate sport leagues have many fewer women than men. The *Can I Play?* report found that women do not participate in intramural athletics in proportion to their numbers. (There may be a relationship between the names given to men's and women's teams and the seriousness with which they are treated — for example, the Carleton University Robins and Ravens and the University of Waterloo Athenas and Warriors. Guess which are the women's teams.) In 1982–83, of over 50 000 students who participated in sports segregated by sex, only 28 per cent were women. This is certainly due, at least in part, to the fact that far larger proportions of the intramural budgets are allocated to male-designated than to female-designated sports. Of over $200 000 spent in 1982–83, only 23 per cent went to women's activities. The imbalance in funding occurs because more sports and more expensive sports (such as hockey and football) are offered for men than for women. For instance, in the fall of 1987 the University of Toronto offered men the choice of ten intramural leagues, while women were offered only seven (*The Energizer*, Fall, 1987). At the University of Guelph during the fall 1987 and winter 1988 terms, men could enrol in nine men's intramural sports leagues, while women could enrol in only four such women's leagues (*Ontarion*, September 8, 1987). At the University of Calgary, too, women have fewer sports in which to excel than men. In the Athletic Building where awards are mounted on the wall there are sixteen possible sports available for men but only eleven for women. In intramural and intercollegiate competition, women may be allowed to play on men's teams if a comparable women's league is not offered, but few women are willing or able to combat the obstacles to their participation. The situation has improved since the 1890s when the request of women at Queen's that they be exempt from paying athletic fees since there were no athletic facilities for them was refused (Neatby, 1978, p. 208). However similarities to that century-old situation remain: although women at all Canadian universities pay as much in athletic fees as men do, they are offered less for this money.

Disparity of opportunity occurs again at the intercollegiate level. Of over 4300 Ontario students participating in intercollegiate sports, only 36 per cent were women. This is hardly surprising in that of over $2.3 million spent by the 12 Ontario universities, women's activities received only 33 per cent of total funding. In athletic meets and competitions, the number of events offered for women is often lower than the number offered for men; a smaller number of events allows a smaller number of participants. As well, men's sports were more likely to have more events (gymnastics, track and field) or larger player rosters (football, ice hockey) (OTFEOA, 1984).

A 1985 in-depth survey of six large Ontario universities indicates the areas in which males are relatively more favored than females (Table 8–1). The total cost of the women's programs was only 32 per cent of the total budget, and the rental costs for sporting facilities only 24 per cent of this budget (Deans of Student Services, Ontario universities, 1986). Although 44 per cent of student participants were women, only 35 per cent of the intercollegiate coaches and the budget for coaching was used for these women.

In the whole of Ontario, about three-quarters of the coaches are men, even though more women than men study physical education in university (OTFEOA, 1984). In the whole of Canada, head coaches of men's programs are nearly always men, and those of women's programs are often men too (Table 8–2). It is disconcerting that the number of women head coaches of women's programs has fallen drastically since 1978, the year the Canadian Women's

Intercollegiate Athletic Union became part of the Canadian Interuniversity Athletic Union (CIAU) (CIAU, 1987).

Table 8–1. Costs and Participation of Athletes and Coaches of Six Ontario Universities* for 22 Intercollegiate Sports

	Total	Percentage Who Are Women or For Women
Coaching costs, salary & benefits	$591 056	35
Total number of non-student coaches	251	35
Programs — total cost	$2 147 223	32
Total number of participants	3 476	44
Regular season travel & meals	$715 097	40
Equipment annual costs	$286 455	34
Facility rental costs	$83 623	24

*McMaster, Queen's, University of Guelph, University of Ottawa, University of Waterloo, University of Western Ontario

— compiled from Ontario Deans of Student Services' Survey, 1985–86

At the time of union, each member institution of the CIAU was allowed two votes rather than one, one to be cast by a person knowledgeable in men's athletics, and one cast by a person knowledgeable in women's athletics (CIAU, 1987). If an institution was unable to send two people to the Annual General Meeting, then one person was empowered to carry two votes. Table 8–2 shows not only that men made up nearly two-thirds of the voting members in 1978, but that their number had increased since then until they comprised 71 per cent in June 1985. In that year a revision of a by-law was passed stating that when two delegates were sent by an institution to the CIAU Annual General Meeting, one should be a woman and one a man. This resulted in 39 per cent of the voting members in 1986 being women (CIAU, 1986), an encouraging trend. Recently, the number of managers, promoters, and head athletic therapists who are women has increased dramatically in Canadian universities, although the women only held 27 per cent of these positions in 1986. The number of women athletes, programs for women, and women athletic administrators has also increased recently, although there are considerably fewer women and women's programs than there are men and men's programs.

Table 8–2. Relative Participation of Women in Canadian Inter-university Athletic Union and its Programs in Two Recent Years

Total Number of Positions and Percentage of Positions Held by Women

	1978–79		1985–86	
	Number	Percentage	Number	Percentage
Athletes	6139	28	7679	30
Programs	389	35	468	40
Head Coaching Positions of Women's Programs				
— full-time	86	76	118	50
— part-time	71	41	99	34
Head Coaching Positions of Men's Programs				
— full-time	149	1	162	1
— part-time	120	1	148	8
Voting Representatives at CIAU Annual Meetings	69	36	79	29
				(1986–87 = 39)
Members of CIAU Committees	53	36	74	43
	1981–82		1985–86	
Athletic Administrators				
— full-time	90	24	121	27
Management and Promotion Positions				
—full-time	26	8	35	26
Head Athletic Therapists				
— full-time	37	5	43	28

— compiled from CIAU, 1987

Awards and scholarships for university athletes benefit men far more than women right across Canada (Table 8–3). Many of these benefits are provided by sources outside the university, such as the federal government, the provincial government and other sports groups, but some are provided by universities, and the universities have made little attempt to ensure that their women and men students have equal access to such money. Nor have they created a climate in which women's athletics are seen to be as important as men's athletics.

The CIAU has not necessarily had a positive effect on women's athletics since the comparable women's and men's bodies joined in 1978. This situation parallels that in secondary schools; as co-educational programs have been introduced into the curricula, more male physical education teachers have begun to teach both girls and boys. The men teachers often have seniority over the women teachers, who leave the school system for a number of reasons including pregnancy and the relocation of their husbands, and the men take over the jobs. It is common for men to teach and coach both girls and boys, but it is seen as inappropriate for women to teach and coach boys (Hall and Richardson, 1982, p. 69).

In addition to systemic discrimination, social factors also contribute to the lower participation rates of women in athletics. Women are given the message, both on campus and off, that women's sports are less important than the better funded, better marketed, and more extensively promoted men's sports. There is also discrimination against female students in the allocation of athletic facilities, practice time, and other services (OTFEOA, 1984; Table 8–1). If women's sports were valued as highly as men's sports, this bias would not exist. Since women have traditionally been excluded from participation in sport (or even vigorous exercise), this message is doubly destructive: not only are old imbalances not being redressed, but new imbalances are being created. Many women are still being taught that having developed muscles is "unfeminine," and that certain sports are best not performed by women.

The atmosphere that surrounds many athletic programs may also discourage women from becoming or remaining athletic. Women involved in sports may have to contend with the arguments put forth by male athletes that women aren't as capable as men athletes. Women who are new to sports, or who are beginning an exercise program, may be discomfitted by the attitudes of some male athletes, attitudes that endorse the division of people into permanent categories of fit and unfit. For example, many university weight training rooms are used mostly

Table 8–3. Awards and Scholarships to Athletes at Canadian Universities, 1984–85

	Atlantic Provinces	Ontario	Manitoba & Saskatchewan	Alberta & British Columbia	Total
Total number of athletes receiving awards	363	460	300	1182	2305
Percentage of these who were women	41	39	33	34	36
Total amount of money of awards reported	$359 737	$882 472	$235 799	$1 243 965	$2 721 973
Percentage of money going to women	37	39	38	35	37
Number of out-of-province athletes with awards	159	41	33	11	244
Percentage of these who were women	33	49	12	18	32

— compiled from AGM Minutes, CIAU, 1985

by men who are experienced with weight training; a woman who is beginning a weight training program may have her efforts ridiculed and minimized by male athletes. A woman student at Carleton University was particularly disturbed when she saw a man in the weight rooms wearing a McGill University Rugby Team T-shirt celebrating "100 years of abusing women (1884–1984)" (*Charlatan,* May 29, 1986). And all women, regardless of their athletic ability, are open to sexual harassment during sport participation, harassment that at best renders such activity unpleasant.

The division of athletic activity into sports suitable to men and sports suitable to women unnecessarily restricts the athletic experience of all participants. No sports should exclude any person, regardless of sex. Also dangerous is the division between the athletic and the unathletic. Exercise and partaking in sport is a part of life that should be accessible to all; yet destructive attitudes about the appropriateness of athletic behavior according to a person's sex, weight, or previous athletic participation encourage the unathletic to so remain, while elevating the athletic to undeserved heights. If women do not participate in sports, they will be unfit for strenuous jobs, more likely to believe in the myth of feminine physical weakness, less likely to be successful in team work, and more likely to be victims of violence. One study showed that women who had played contact sports such as football were less likely than other women to be raped (Bart, 1987). Athleticism should not be a gift bestowed on a privileged few or a title to be earned through conspicuous participation in popular sports; it should be a right possessed by all.

Chapter 9
Sexism, Sexual Harassment, and Violence

When I started university I was excited and I thought I was
going to a place where women and men would be equal.
Obscene pictures of naked women are carved in the library
carrels. Posters of voluptuous women are pinned to the lab
walls. One science building shows photos of the university's
66 top physicists, every single one of them a man. My only
woman teacher is a part-time lecturer, while all of the full
professors in my faculty are men. I try to find women
academics to learn from as role models; most of the women
I've been able to find are secretaries, cafeteria workers, and
the "housekeeper" who cleans my room. Hanging statues in
one of the buildings feature a man and women; the man's
limbs are free but the women's legs are tied tightly together
along their length. I wonder what symbolism the artist
had in mind when he made the work, and what the
university has in mind displaying it.

Chris
Second-year student, 1987

Sexist Atmosphere

Sexual harassment and violence against women are the most obvious manifestations of the sexist attitude present in Canadian
universities. Although many women do not become victims of
these crimes during their university careers, all university women
are subject both to the threat of sex-specific physical violence and
to the more subtle sexism that creates an uncomfortable ambience.
This atmosphere can affect women students' ability to concentrate,
hamper their freedom to work, and destroy or thwart the creation of a supportive environment. Yet despite the impact of a sexist
ambience on the quality of university women's lives, its existence
most often goes unacknowledged. The feelings that it provokes
in women are denied (doesn't she have a sense of humor?) ridiculed
(what's *your* problem, honey?) or minimized (that's life, be
realistic). The constant, cumulative strain of this atmosphere may
be as disruptive as the strain of sexual harassment.

Since this environment exists at all universities, the examples that follow can be taken as representative of the experience of Canadian university women.

- Thompson attended a workshop on rape at the University of Waterloo Women's Centre where she learned a great deal that could help her if she were assaulted, and also things she could do to help others. When she went back to her classes afterward and mentioned to a male "friend" that she had been to a workshop on rape, he replied, "Did they teach you how to do it?"

- The posters for another workshop, this time on sexual harassment, were torn down soon after they were put up. When Thompson went to this workshop, she was surprised to find that the two people who were to show a film and lead the discussion were men. Wouldn't it have been more appropriate to have at least one woman leading the group, since women are most affected by sexual harassment?, she wondered. After the film, when there were no further questions for discussion, one of the leaders joked, "Good, because I don't know what to do about it [sexual harassment], I just know how to do it."

- At Carleton University there are tunnels that connect almost all of the buildings on the campus. Each year, the residences have a big competition to paint the best mural in the tunnels. The murals are generally in bad taste and very often sexist; there are always several that are misogynist. One year, the Women's Centre lobbied to get the worst of the murals painted over and to make sure they weren't produced again. There were many arguments in *favor* of the sexist murals, the essence of which was that freedom of expression is more important than offending a few sensitive women. As recently as February 1987, several years after that incident, sexist posters were still being painted on the walls of the tunnels, and their artists continue to defend them on the basis of freedom of expression.

- At the University of Waterloo, where two professors are close friends, technicians refer to the more eminent professor not by name but as the other professor's "girl."

- In the University of Waterloo's Graphics Services, the employees refused to typeset a poem about incest by a woman because they found it too gross.

- The graffiti found in hallways, on desks, on library carrels, and anywhere else people can write it, is particularly misogynist and out of place at an institute of higher learning. People write

CENSORED

This page originally contained graffiti from university library walls. Even though women experience such visual violence every day, the publisher was advised that to print the truth would be politically too sensitive. Therefore the graffiti has been censored.

graffiti because they want to share information with others; this information is usually that women are made for sex with men and must not forget it.

- Despite the use of the non-sexist term "frosh" at some universities to denote first-year students, the atmosphere in the residences themselves is anything but non-sexist. For instance:

  - Women are treated as sexual objects on posters. A recent one displayed at Trinity College, Toronto, to advertise a party pictured a scantily clad woman with lettering across her chest and crotch. On her forehead was a question mark, indicating that what the woman is thinking or feeling is irrelevant, incomprehensible, or non-existent. Printed below were the words, "Put Strange Things on the Face" (*The Varsity,* January 26, 1987).
  - A McGill University fraternity poster portrayed a gang rape scene in which the victim seemed to be enjoying the experience.
  - In a student dormitory at the University of Waterloo, posters advertising parties often refer to women and men with different words. The terms used, such as doctor/nurses, skiers/skibunnies, and cucumbers/tacos, are often derogatory to women. Such posters often note that women can get in for less money than men, because more women are needed to make the party a success.

- At the University of Toronto, first-year men are initiated each fall into Victoria College with the Men's Traditional Ceremonies (MTC). These involve kneeling down and kissing a piece of carpet soaked in fish oil and splattered with chicken blood called a "muff," and representing a large vagina. The symbolism is emphasized by the presence at the ceremony of a large inflated female doll. The ritual was led in 1986 by abusive leaders who instigated "yelling, burping and insulting." Some frosh were unperturbed by the ceremony, but many were upset — two were thrown out and one threw up in response to it (*The Strand,* March 13, 1987). There is talk at present of changing the ceremony to something less disgusting. It would copy the women's ceremony, which is not "vulgarities performed on a giant phallus," but rather a quiet, candle-lit meeting where the women are told about the college's traditions. Andrea Williams does not agree with men who think the MTC is a lark:

  The reality of the matter is this: women are raped and beaten every day, or, on a less overtly violent level, seen as sex objects

97

and valued only in terms of their potential to satisfy men. And yes, I do take rape, assault, and sexual harassment seriously. The very fact that such a ceremony exists or existed at Vic within living memory is proof that we are not yet in a position to laugh at sexism, or more specifically, overt manifestations of misogyny. (p. 3)

- At a morning orientation event at the University of Toronto in September 1987, about 25 engineering students on their way to Convocation Hall passed a life-sized inflated female doll from hand to hand, shoved a beer bottle in and out between its legs, then threw it to the ground where several men jumped on it in simulated rape. On that same campus, during the same week, one woman was sexually attacked, while another was physically assaulted by a group of male students. Both women were treated at hospital emergency wards.

- At some universities, the engineering students have stag parties throughout the year. Every term, the main welcome-back event is a stag subsidized by the student society. (Women are often expected to organize their own events without the help of the student society.)

- Stag parties also occur during graduation celebrations. At one university, in 1985, to accommodate the growing number of female graduate students, a male burlesque show was introduced to complement the usual female strippers. The next year, the issue became so controversial that the graduating students held a vote to decide whether to do away with the strippers or to have both male and female strippers. The result was 51 per cent in favor of the show; despite extensive boycotting, it went on as planned.

- Sexist pranks are a favorite of engineering students. For example, students dressed a female manikin taken into a University of Waterloo study room in a gas mask, men's neck ties on its breasts, lace panties, and a see-through shawl. At the same university, the engineers' mascot is a giant wrench called the Rigid Tool. The University of British Columbia and Lakehead University Engineering Societies both defend fiercely their right to have a nude Lady Godiva on their logo (*Iron Warrior*, University of Waterloo, January 1987).

- Engineering newspapers in Canada are so embarrassing to universities and to the engineering profession that these arsenals against women have been banned on several campuses, and at the University of Saskatchewan, the editors were charged under the Human Rights Act and required to take courses to improve their morals.

Engineering newspapers are notorious for their misogynist content, but mainstream campus newspapers are far from innocent. For example:

- The sports section of a University of Toronto student newspaper contained an article about the great contribution that the "ladies" of the *Sports Illustrated* Annual Swimsuit Issue make to the world (*The New Edition,* February 3, 1987).
- Another student newspaper ran a contest in which the winner selected the best model of swimsuits (*The Newspaper,* U of T, March 11, 1987).
- *The Gargoyle* (University College, Toronto, February 27, 1987) included a reprinted borderline pornographic short story in which the only female character is depicted as a demon who seduces an innocent young man; the young man becomes sexually aroused when the female character mysteriously becomes covered with blood. The story is illustrated by voluptuous naked women crouching like animals.
- Many newspapers carry advertisements from travel agencies that feature pictures of scantily clad women sitting on a beach, or drawings of naked women (*Lexicon,* York University, April, 1987).
- The University of Toronto's *The Newspaper* carried an advertisement for a pornographic cinema, and featured the cinema's hot-line number, which played a breathy female voice climaxing in orgasm. Students had to fight the newspaper to have the ad removed, and it was included in the newspaper even after its editors had agreed not to carry it (*Otherwise,* University of Toronto, November 25, 1986).
- A classified advertisement section of the University of Waterloo's *Imprint* included a message which advocated stepping on a woman's face if she did not obey orders to provide beer.
- An ad in the Wilfrid Laurier University student newspaper advises readers to "Show your enthusiasm, get out there and belt your spouse" (*The Cord,* October 22, 1987).

• Dagg recently sat on an all-women committee formed to decide how to reward teachers who use non-sexist language and gender-balanced material in their courses. We had all been so intimidated in the past that we rejected the name Egalitarian

Award as too controversial. We decided that no matter what its name, it would have to be carefully promoted: otherwise some teachers, fearing a backlash from conservative colleagues, might not want to receive it.

Sexist Professors

Sexist behavior by professors is not as blatant as it used to be, with professors addressing classes of women and men students as "Gentlemen" or inserting slides of naked women into their illustrated lectures, but it is still pervasive. General examples of "ordinary" sexism include:

- The use of derogatory terms against women in general. One psychology professor told his students that a theory he was describing was so simple "even a housewife could understand it."

- The use of "humorous" comments to demean or trivialize women. A philosopher talking about sociobiology mentions the "raving feminists" who do not agree with his ideas. Another ends his lecture on Aristotle's views of women with "but we all know one thing women are good for."

- The telling of sexist jokes about women even though professors now often preface such jokes with "I know this is sexist. . . ." Such remarks are doubly offensive, because in making them the professor acknowledges that such stories are hurtful, but in telling the story he shows that he does not care.

- The reinforcing of sexist stereotypes. Some professors of business refer to "businessmen" supported in their work by secretaries who are "girls." Women are told by a professor discussing a societal problem that "all this has happened because you girls aren't at home doing what you're supposed to be doing." A teacher has so many pin-up pictures of voluptuous women on his office walls that students refuse to visit him there.

- The use of women as sexual objects, often to make a point. An engineering professor pretends not to notice large posters of a nearly naked woman on the lecture hall walls. A geology professor calls one of his women students "cleavage" while discussing the geological concept of the same name. An English professor explains the effectiveness of using a surprise ending by saying "we all know that a partially clad woman is more attractive than a completely naked woman." A psychology lecturer, in explaining the power of positive thinking, shows an overhead of a drawing of two men's heads. One man's brow is furrowed and the drawing of the convolutions of his brain has angular lines, while the other man is smiling — his brain tissue convolutions are in the shape of women's breasts. An English professor in a large first-year lecture on power has a scantily clothed bellydancer, with her hands apparently tied together, led down the aisle at the end of a rope. He then dances with her briefly and makes some lewd comments about marriage. When women in the class object to this performance, he apologizes that he is "a dirty old man." At the next class he gives each of them a rose. A physics professor reads out a problem to his first-year mechanics course which involves a prince using a ladder to rescue Princess Griselda, who has, "even though she was only a princess, a queen-size bosom (115 lbs. of nubile pulchritude)." He reads that "her hand (and other choice portions of her anatomy) had been promised to the king of a nearby country." (This "Static Fairy Tale" had appeared in *Phys 13 News,* which is sent to all Ontario high schools. It is not surprising that few high school girls choose to study physics at university.)

- The continual use of sexist language. Many professors still use generic masculine terms like "he" or "man," and speak of "Neanderthal Man," "Economic Man," and "Technological Man." This usage reinforces students' impression that men are the important people in society, and that women are, and should be, insignificant. In geography and sociology, expressions such as "farmers and their wives" and "immigrants and their wives" are routinely used. These expressions are inaccurate and imply that women are not, and cannot be, farmers or immigrants. Students are encouraged in this way to think that "male" is the normal state of being, as in "farmer" or "immigrant," and that "female" is abnormal and incomplete — a woman can only be a "wife." One woman who complained to a professor about his exclusive use of male pronouns was told that she should not bother herself with such "trivial" questions. When she questioned an accounting professor who referred to a manager as "he," however, he reacted with anger and emotion, arguing that women had to be kept in their place or they would take over the world.

- The use of misogynist material in lectures. One professor bases much of his philosophy course on anti-choice for abortion material. When one of his disgruntled students wrote an article exposing the course's blatant bias, the student newspaper refused to publish it.

Extensive studies have showed that many teachers treat their male students more seriously than their female students (Spender, 1982). They call on men more often than women in class discussions, they interrupt women more or allow others to do so, they give men's ideas more serious consideration than women's, and they treat women who ask extensive questions or challenge stereotypes as troublemakers (Hall and Sandler, 1982; Franklin, 1981). Such treatment creates a serious educational disadvantage for women, as we noted earlier.

Some professors feel so strongly about their right to ignore feminist scholarship that they continue to submit material to university calendars that is sexually biased. Texts include the student being always male ("student . . . his") and the confusing use of "man" to mean both the human male and the species *Homo sapiens*. Research shows that when the generic form of "man" is used, people almost always think of male people, rather than of women and men equally, which is why feminists avoid this use (Miller and Swift, 1976). At the University of Waterloo, Dagg (1984b) publicized the various departments which had calendar submissions that used sexist language or language that was misleading. Many of them changed their wording in subsequent calendars, but some did not. Courses listed in the 1987–88 undergraduate calendar include Man–Machine Communications (engineering), Man and Nature (Environment and Resource Studies, formerly the Man–Environment Department), From Matter to Man, The Seas and Man's Effects upon Them, and The Inland Waters and Man's Effects upon Them (science), Man in Crisis (Literary Views), Man in Crisis 1, and Man in Crisis 2 (arts courses with all-male reading lists; what, one wonders, about women in crises?), and Philosophy of Man (philosophy).

Many universities allow or encourage businesses in need of personnel to go to their campuses to interview students. These companies often want to hire men over women and make their wishes clear. One engineering student was told by an interviewer in 1986 that the chemical engineering job she was applying for was not suitable for "girls." An arts student was told that she had childbearing hips and should go home and have a baby. The women do not know how many other positions were denied them because they are female.

That employers use a person's gender in their hiring decisions is evident in the university classes given to help students find summer jobs. Interview-training sessions informing students about how to respond to questions and which mannerisms to avoid always include a segment on personal appearance. Female students are taught that their chances of getting a job are best if they wear skirts, and they are discouraged from wearing pants. Male students, however, are told only to dress neatly.

Treatment of Feminists

Feminists, who want to improve society for all of us, are profoundly threatening to many women and men who like things the way they are. Feminists at universities are especially unwelcome because universities are so conservative. If a feminist professor nevertheless decides to maintain and express her views in her work, she may well face criticism that her work is not scholarly, or that she is not being objective. We have seen that few women are hired as professors and given tenure, and feminists are a minute fraction of these.

It is difficult to be a feminist when one's ideas are so often met with hate and derision. One lecturer who taught a course on women's history found that her greatest opposition came from her administrative assistant. The lecturer was badgered about such things as the number of photocopies she made. The assistant did not share the lecturer's views about women, and tried her hardest to thwart the lecturer's efforts (personal communication, February 16, 1987).

The case of Sheila McIntyre discussed earlier emphasizes that students as well as faculty have considerable power in determining the treatment a feminist teacher receives. Students' actions can range from simply annoying disagreement and argument about feminist questions to violent acts such as destroying property. The classroom climate can be made unworkable through attempts to discredit the teacher by questioning her expertise, or discounting her views — "She's just a feminist, she's not worth listening to." Students sometimes boycott classes, ridicule feminist teachers in public, or use course evaluations to direct their anger at a particular teacher through her supervisors.

Feminist students who witness these activities are made to feel uncomfortable. They are even more upset when they themselves are targetted for abuse. Feminist students may be ignored by their peers, have their views dismissed as radical, and be ridiculed and ostracized. Anti-feminist professors also contribute to the difficulty

103

of feminist students' lives. A student's views may be dismissed as being emotional and partisan. She may be branded as a fanatic, and not considered equally with other students for employment or study positions. As one professor stated it, "I have no time for strident feminists." Apart from the problems of being singled out and subjected to sarcasm, feminist students may face academic hurdles if a professor does not give credit for work done from a feminist perspective, or penalizes students for presenting feminist analyses which do not mirror the professor's opinion on a question.

Many students are angered by the spectre of non-sexist language. A student who commented on a male colleague's reference to God as "He" was hostilely asked why she and other feminists wasted time on useless feminist rhetoric, even though several organized religions are now questioning their own creation of male images of God. In a seminar where one male professor was corrected by another on his use of the term "man" to refer to humanity, most of the students responded with a groan. Some expressed the opinion that the professor who made the correction was being unreasonably critical.

Such negative reactions to what is only balanced and fair undermines many women's zeal (which is presumably what is wanted). When Sheila McIntyre's women students encountered their male colleagues' bias against feminists, they were at first shocked and then galvanized by it. They believed that when they exposed this prejudice and spoke against it, they would be able to bring about egalitarian change. They were bold and full of optimism. As the weeks went by, however, and the anti-women sentiments did not die out, they lost heart. One woman was labelled a lesbian, then shunned and discredited. At least three others were trivialized or silenced by their teachers who made feminist-baiting jokes, ignored their questions, and allowed no class time for discussion of the implications of sexist practice. Two women began to skip classes. The most energetic reformist dissented less often: "She stopped talking in class and occasionally spoke to her teachers in private about remarks she had found offensive, but she did so jokingly and appeasingly." Without exception, the students who had consulted with McIntyre about how to promote equality in law school began to ask her about ways to survive the program. Three feminist students thought seriously about dropping law (McIntyre, 1987, p. 9).

A feminist graduate student at Queen's has had the courage to express, albeit anonymously, her own dissatisfaction with her education because of Sheila McIntyre's memo (Anon., 1987, pp. 4–6) One of her male professors was pleased with her work until she began to pursue feminist ideas in her term paper and ask pointed questions in class. Then he spoke against her to a colleague, called her "stupid" and a "dolt," and threatened to fail her in his course despite her better-than-average standing in her year. He finally admitted that he did not "hit it off intellectually or personally" with this woman, although she did not see why this was relevant.

In 1986, this student became a teaching assistant. When one of the readings in the course to which she was assigned contained an item relating to women, one of the other T.A.s came to her to ask how she planned to deal with it. When she told him, he said, "That gender stuff is crap." She asked the professor to give the class some idea of the significance of women's role in the topic of study, and he did so by saying their involvement was "limited to womanlike activities such as making tea." When she later objected, the professor refused to discuss his curt dismissal of women with her.

In a particularly virulent letter against feminists, an assistant geology professor at Queen's lumps fascists and feminists together, claims that by hiring feminists academic freedom is destroyed, compares the Keegstra affair to feminists offering their version of current and historical events, and argues that the "student's birthright to freedom of thought and the free examination of ideas should, and indeed must," protest this usurpation of academic privilege by the feminist organization (Toogood, 1987).

A subsequent letter to the *Queen's Journal* by Will Kymlicka (1987) points out that

- women's studies courses are *not* necessarily taught by feminists,
- political variations are as great among feminists as among non-feminists,
- feminists have studied women to some extent and are surely thus more qualified to teach women's studies courses than teachers who have no such expertise,
- feminists are not seeking a monopoly on knowledge; they encourage women's studies because non-feminists have not considered women *worth* studying in most disciplines. Feminists are not trying to take over forums in which women are discussed, they are trying to *create* forums in which they *can* be discussed,
- if the geologist had been genuinely concerned with free expression, he would have supported Sheila McIntyre instead of attacking her with fabrications,

- if he were truly concerned about discrimination in hiring practices, he would have been worried about discrimination against feminists,

- if he respected the dignity of others, he would not have originally published his letter in a paper which admits to being sexist.

Even women professors sometimes write to university papers urging that no program to help women be considered, since merit is all that matters in hiring and promoting. One such woman "publicly laments that we do women's studies and mainstreaming only because we are in academic life through affirmative action. We are to be pitied, as well as judged, because in our heart of hearts we know that our place in academic life is unmerited and unearned" (Stimpson, 1984, p. 23). This pathetic undervaluation of women's work undermines her own and every woman's work.

The pages of student publications, too, are sprinkled with letters from feminists urging some reform or objecting to some sexist practice, followed by angry responses from anti-feminist students. For example, in the fall of 1986, the Women's Centre Collective (WCC) at the University of Toronto indicated that it would be monitoring campus newspapers for sexist content and for their coverage of events of interest to women. It had found that women were not equally represented with men in these papers (not really a surprise), and felt they should be. It offered to suggest ways in which campus coverage could be improved.

The reaction to this announcement was outrage. Whereas the Women's Centre Collective had used words such as "giving public recognition," "inform," and "educate," the editorial in the November *Innis Herald* entitled "Nice Ass" accused the Collective of attempting "to remove the freedom of the press," of "censorship," and of saying that "editorial freedom must be quashed." The editorial goes on to say that the *Innis Herald* is tempted to "sever all ties" with the WCC: "This would include refusal to publish promotional material or to provide coverage of Women's Centre sponsored events." To most people this looks remarkably like the censorship that journalists are so anxious to prevent for themselves.

As another example, a feminist journalist at the University of Waterloo was attacked verbally because she objected to the sexist engineering newspaper *Enginews*. A woman engineer wrote to the student newspaper about the journalist: "Anyone that paranoid must be riddled with ulcers and back pain from looking over her shoulder. Better lay off the coke, sister." (*Imprint,* February 22, 1985).

The anti-feminist presence at universities is so pervasive that it affects all women. When women at the University of Waterloo gathered a few years ago to found the Professional Women's Association to address common concerns, one theme which predominated was that the group must not be openly political. Most women agreed that sexual discrimination existed at the university, but there was no consensus that such discrimination should be addressed openly. The women were desperately anxious that their group not have a negative image and that it not do anything the least bit radical. One professor was highly amused at the name of this group, because he claimed that "professional women" meant prostitutes (personal communication).

Sexual Harassment

Sexual harassment mars the experience of many university women. Sexual harassment is becoming well-known in universities as well as elsewhere as a pervasive but under-reported problem. Responses to a survey by the BC Public Interest Research Group at Simon Fraser University (Burger, 1986) indicated that of 444 women who returned questionnaires (53 per cent of those who received them):

- 50 per cent of undergraduates had been sexually harassed, often by other students,
- 61 percent of graduate students had been sexually harassed, mostly by faculty,
- 33 per cent of all students had been subjected to discriminatory remarks related to their sex,
- 25 per cent had experienced inappropriate staring or leering at their body,
- 14 per cent had had to look at suggestive material in the educational setting,
- 11 per cent had reported inappropriate advances suggesting sexual intimacy,
- 4 per cent had been sexually assaulted.

However, only 11 per cent of respondents who experienced sexual harassment recognized it as such, and only 2 per cent had reported their experience to some university authority. The

107

university has no policy or procedures for dealing with sexual harassment.

Sexual harassment can take many forms, as the following examples indicate:

- A professor at McMaster constantly refers to sex in class examples and jokes: he asks female students about their sexual experiences and seems to go out of his way to make them feel ill-at-ease.

- An English instructor's comments about women make a female student uncomfortable. While discussing an incident of sexual assault in a novel, the instructor says that the character "deserved what she got." The student protests, but the instructor replies, looking at her breasts, "Well, if she looks like you do, I'm sure he couldn't help himself" (Chimming, 1986, p. 21).

- An engineering professor tells a student who is inquiring about a summer job that he doesn't usually hire "girls," and asks if she is trying to look sexy by not wearing a bra; as she leaves he calls out, "You'll have to come over for a feel sometime."

Sexual harassment can cause a victim embarrassment, humiliation, and other stress which interferes with her performance at university. If the victim is a student, her marks and academic future may be affected by a professor's behavior; if she is a faculty member, tenure or even her job may be threatened because she does not comply with her harasser's demands. Research at the University of Waterloo under Professor Susan McDaniel is being carried out to investigate the effect of sexual harassment on other areas of the victim's physical and mental health.

Data are being collected in universities across Canada on the extent of sexual harassment, on ways to deal with it most effectively, and on its effects. Education programs and mechanisms to help victims are increasingly being devised and mounted. In 1980, York University was the first in Canada to give official recognition to the problem (CAUT *Bulletin,* November 1986). By April 1987, the University of British Columbia and Simon Fraser University were described as being "among the few universities in Canada which do not have formal procedures to handle sexual harassment complaints" (CAUT *Bulletin,* April, 1987).

Recently, a woman student who felt she was a victim of sexual harassment at Simon Fraser University took her case to the British Columbia courts in July 1987 (*The Peak,* Simon Fraser University, July 16–22, 1987). A professor, Lenard Cohen, had hired her to prepare the index of his book for him. Between

November 3 and November 25, 1986, this woman's residence received a number of anonymous phone calls of a harassing nature which were traced to Cohen's home phone. On November 17, the woman sent Cohen a letter of termination from his project. That same day her residence received 27 calls within an hour and a half from Cohen's home, and the next evening a further 14 calls. Cohen defended his conduct by saying in court that he wanted to make sure his book was returned, and that he had had difficulty getting in touch with his helper. The judge acquitted him, concluding that "the defendent is . . . a professor in good standing with a good reputation . . . who has standards that are particularly stringent." *The Peak* editor observes that Cohen was acquitted because he is "a professional in good standing at SFU and therefore must be telling the truth." This precedent — every professor is a professional and has credibility, and students and others who find the professor's conduct unacceptable do not — is unfortunate and dangerous.

The design of sexual harassment policies is not without controversy; the University of Toronto has recently been embroiled in a debate over the length of time appropriate for reporting incidents of sexual harassment. Students and staff argue that the period must be at least as long as the longest course, so that a student victim can obtain a mark in a course before confronting the professor who harassed her and who might otherwise express his displeasure by lowering her grade. The Faculty Association, which realizes that its members are likely to include most sexual harassers, wants a two-month limit. In May, 1987, even though 90 per cent of the university community wanted a six-month limit, the university ruled in its new policy that complaints of harassment must be filed within four months of the date of the alleged incident, with possible rare exceptions to six months (U of T *Bulletin,* May 25, 1987).

Even if a university has a sexual harassment policy in place, it does not mean that much can be done about the problem. Where the faculty is unionized, as at York University, there is little hope of ever forcing a professor to stop harassing his students if he wishes to do so. Indeed, for a non-involved person even to appear before a committee involved with sexual harassment may result in extreme penalties, as Mary Warner discovered at Brock University in the case described earlier.

Sexual Violence

Sexual violence is not perceived by many non-feminists at Canadian universities as an issue. During May 1987, the campus of the University of Toronto was festooned with a poster depicting a male raping a female cartoon character and advertizing a "Best of Sex and Violence Cartoon Festival." Among provocative female cartoon characters are the words, "You'll be amazed how much you missed as a kid." How long would similar posters about Jews and Violence, or Blacks and Violence, have been tolerated?

All women are subject to violent attacks because of their sex. In the 1985–86 academic year, 235 incidents of violence, including physical and sexual assault, were reported on ten Ontario campuses. A study done by the Canadian Advisory Council on the Status of Women revealed that two-thirds of the victims in 178 Ontario sexual assault cases were students (*Charlatan,* Carleton University, February 5, 1987).

The incidents of sexual assault and violence against women on university campuses range from severe sexual harassment to murder. Some women always choose times when other people are in the vicinity to visit a certain professor's office. Students warn their friends about professors who make sexual advances to women students and suggest that if possible they keep these men from closing their office doors. Many women fear being alone at night on certain parts of their campuses because incidents of sexual assault have occurred there. Crime can occur in any place at any time, however. A McMaster classics professor who had been working in her office on a Sunday morning was murdered by a man in 1983 (*Globe and Mail,* January 30, 1984). Following this tragedy, the McMaster Security Director warned students that they were taking a risk if they walked alone on campus or worked in offices late at night. Women's groups objected that possible victims were being held responsible for potential crimes. Many women did restrict their movements on campus at night, which made it even more deserted than usual and consequently also less safe.

Despite the high incidence of violence against women across Canada, the safety of women students is seldom a priority of university administrations. Although students sometimes request the release of statistics and locations of reported incidents so that women can be informed and act to protect themselves, security offices may refuse to release this information, fearing that it would give the university a bad name. As a result, many women are left unaware of the extent of the problem, and of potentially dangerous areas. Even so, women usually avoid isolated areas on university grounds at night, especially when the lighting is inadequate or nonexistent. When the lamps in lonely areas are

110

either removed or not turned on, security offices have denied knowledge of the lack of lighting and have not taken the matter seriously.

A study completed at Carleton University itemizes what areas the 114 female student respondents perceived to be unsafe (Leach et al., 1986). (Male students were not included in the research because most felt no fear while on campus.) The three most cited reasons for fear after dark were poor lighting (mentioned 60 times), isolation or few people about (mentioned 63 times), and the possibility of hiding places, such as bushes and trees (mentioned 14 times). Many women refused to use the tunnels at night, and found them especially threatening when there was graffiti on the walls. Others would not use the often apparently deserted six-storey parking garage which has limited exits.

Although women who have cars are in less danger than those who must walk at night, women who drive are by no means safe. Parking lots are often far away from the buildings where night classes are held, or from the library. In efforts to park in safe areas which are not a long dark walk from where they are going, some women park in no parking zones. When one woman, whose car was ticketed, asked the security officer who had given her the ticket where she should park in order to be close to her destination, he treated her as though she were making unreasonable demands. The male officer would not understand her concern about the fifteen-minute walk to the parking lot.

Even though some campus security offices downplay the question of women's safety on university campuses, their actions indicate their recognition of cause for concern. Violent incidents have been reported in underground walking tunnels at several universities across Canada. Sections of these tunnels have been permanently closed at many universities; some are closed at night, or on weekends and holidays. One of the two main entrances to the Ontario Institute for Studies in Education, in the middle of downtown Toronto, has closed every night at six o'clock since a woman was raped in the bushes near that entrance (personal communication, January 21, 1988). Obviously, though public admission of any problem is rare, universities know that their grounds are not safe places for women.

Regardless of whether the question of violence against women is fully acknowledged by university administrations, it does affect the quality of life of university women. The threat of sexual assault impairs the freedom of women to work late, take evening courses, attend extra-curricular events, or accept night jobs on campus. Though information has been best documented at Simon

Fraser, it is not the only university where, in response to possible violence, women have taken assertiveness training courses, learned self-defence techniques, worn unattractive clothing, used the available escort system, organized a buddy system, and carried spraycans to protect themselves (Burger, 1986).

Chapter 10
What's To Be Done

Men will have to abandon the concept of objectivity which they have erected and appropriated for themselves, and accept the limitations of their own subjectivity. . .

Dale Spender
Invisible Women: The Schooling Scandal, 1982

So far, we have pointed out many of the things that are sexist, and therefore wrong, in Canadian universities. There has been progress in fighting misogyny in some areas at some campuses, however, and in this chapter we will suggest how conditions generally could be improved. Where possible, we cite examples of progress that Canadian universities could emulate.

Realities of Student Life (Chapter 1)

Women students should be encouraged to enrol and remain in disciplines where there are few women, such as engineering, physics, and geology. Universities could help both undergraduate and graduate students cultivate mentors who would help them succeed in their academic careers. This might involve peer advising programs, information on unwritten policies and practices, support organizations, and informal discussion groups (see Simeone, 1987, p. 110, and Haley, 1985, p. 158). Mentors might be willing to help students publish articles and papers.

Haley recommends also for graduate students that:

- Professors and graduate secretaries be given special training in order to become sensitized to students' needs, especially in their first year.

- Departmental monies be divided to cover each student's basic living costs. Scholarships would then provide supplements to this basic income.

- Professors and teaching assistants attend seminars to learn important concepts from adult education theory.

- Universities be reorganized so that their priority is developing whole individuals rather than students who are interested only in competitive research.
- Universities monitor the progress of graduate students so that if some fall behind, the reasons for this can be determined and problem areas can be identified and corrected.

The Council of Ontario Universities advises similar measures (*Committee News*, May, 1987).

Teaching and Course Content (Chapters 2–4)

Professors who wish to eliminate sexual discrimination in the classroom can work toward their goal by:

- Not making generalized statements about girls or women that merely reflect society's bias, such as "women are less rational than men."
- Not making jokes that belittle or demean women, such as "we all know what women are good for,"
- Using non-sexist language in order to portray women and men as equals.
- Avoiding illustrations that reflect society's bias and allocation of status, with bosses always men and secretaries women.

Professors can address classroom discrimination more positively by:

- Choosing course material that treats both women and men equally. If there is less material available on women than men, or if a discipline is founded upon what men rather than women have done and thought, then this gender imbalance should be explained and discussed with the class.
- Reinforcing rather than ridiculing women who use new language (such as "herstory"), or want to study feminist material (such as that dealing with goddesses or incest), or object to sexism in courses.
- Ensuring that non-sexist textbooks, if they are available, are prescribed for courses.
- Reading some of the thousands of available books on gender rather than asking women to explain what they mean or want.
- Encouraging their departments to add a question to student evaluations-of-teaching forms concerning discriminatory behaviour in the classroom.

114

- Having a neutral observer monitor the treatment of women and men in the classroom — are they allowed to answer questions equally? Are women interrupted more than men? Are questions addressed as much to women as men?

No Canadian university has yet taken formal measures to avoid sexism in the classroom (Black, 1987). Specific recommendations to improve conditions for women in medical schools are given in *Murmurs of the Heart* (Support Group, 1985, p. 35).

York University has made a special effort to attract girls to physics by having an annual Christmas lecture for grade 9 and 10 students, half girls, from nearby high schools. In addition, it has recently held three-day residential workshops for girls in this age group where they learn to make an AM/FM radio, teach a spider to spin a web with which to catch water droplets that can be seen and photographed in a microscope, and make a laser hologram. The faculty is hoping that the girls who participate will want to continue taking physics and math throughout their high school career. York is helped in these endeavors by the group WISH, Women In Science, Hopefully (Megaw, 1986).

Women's Studies (Chapter 5)

Women's studies should be an accepted discipline at universities with the same status and budget control as the traditional disciplines. It should offer graduate programs where feminists can be trained in a broad base of subjects that enables them to become professors specializing in this field. Few, if any, universities in Canada have adequate budgets for their women's studies programs. Most of the courses are taught in the traditional departments, so there is little control over their content, over who teaches them, or even whether they are offered on a regular basis. Research now being undertaken will document what women's studies courses and courses taught from a feminist perspective have been given in Canadian universities (contact Margrit Eichler, Ontario Institute for Studies in Education, Toronto).

Important backing for women's studies in Canada has occurred with the creation in 1983–84 of the Endowment Assistance Program for Chairs in Women's Studies by the Secretary of State. These chairs are to provide impetus for multidisciplinary teaching and research related to women. The federal government contributes $500 000 toward endowment funds for each chair, and the beneficiary universities match this amount. The five regional

Chairs of Women's Studies, all of which have now been established, are:

1. Simon Fraser University (Pacific Region)
   Chair Holder: Rosemary Brown,
2. Universities of Winnipeg/Manitoba
   (Joint Chairs for the Prairie Region)
   Chair Holder: Keith Louise Fulton,
3. Carleton University/University of Ottawa
   (Joint Chairs for Ontario)
   Chair Holder: Monique Bégin,
4. Laval University (Quebec)
   Chair will be in operation by September 1988,
5. Mount Saint Vincent University (Atlantic)
   Chair Holder: Marguerite Andersen.

It is still far too early to determine the effect these chairs will have on women's studies and on universities in general (Marguerite Andersen became the holder of the first established chair in 1987), but the federal government is to be commended for its initiative. The high calibre of the women being chosen to hold these positions makes many women optimistic about the influence the chairs will have. On the other hand, however, it is ominous that the University of Manitoba severely cut its women's studies program in 1986, despite the fact that one of the conditions of endowment is the maintenance at current level of the program (*Herizons,* September, 1986).

Rather than seek to mirror traditional ways of teaching, we believe that new ideas engendered by women's studies should be retained and expanded. The teacher should not pose as the expert, since every woman has important information that increases our knowledge of women in society. Rather, all students should be encouraged to share their experiences. Where possible, course material should be relevant to women's lives, and women should be encouraged to fight social wrongs.

A number of books have been published recently which facilitate the inclusion of information on women in courses. Three such books are *Women's Studies, A Recommended Core Bibliography* (1979), by Esther Stineman, which lists 1763 annotated items; *Half the Sky: An Introduction to Women's Studies* (1979), by the Bristol Women's Studies Group; and the 621-page *Women's Realities, Women's Choices,* by the Hunter College Women's Studies Collective.

Recent Canadian books which are invaluable for a variety of disciplines include:

A Not Unreasonable Claim. Women and Reform in Canada 1880s–1920s (1979) edited by Linda Kealey, which has chapters on sociology and history;

Feminism in Canada: From Pressure to Politics (1982) edited by Angela Miles and Geraldine Finn, which deals with science, psychology, economics, history, anthropology, philosophy, and social work;

Still Ain't Satisfied! (1982) edited by Maureen FitzGerald, Connie Guberman, and Margie Wolfe (sociology, economics, and history);

A World of Difference (1982) by Esther Greenglass (sociology, economics, psychology);

Women, the Family, and the Economy (1982) by S. J. Wilson (sociology, economics, history, political science);

Perspectives on Women in the 1980s (1983) edited by Joan Turner and Lois Emery (sociology, social work, and history);

Knowledge Reconsidered: A Feminist Overview (1984) by Ursula Franklin et al. (ethics, English literature, history, anthropology, sociology, and technology);

Women in Canada. A Bibliography 1965 to 1982 compiled by Carol Mazur and Sheila Pepper (which lists 7584 articles and books, etc., on women);

Rethinking Canada. The Promise of Women's History (1986) edited by Veronica Strong-Boag and Anita Clair Fellman.

Somer Brodribb (1987) lists many more books about women in Canada, several of which will be published in 1988, and the Canadian Women's Periodical Index Project will finish its retrospective index of the most widely used Canadian feminist periodicals in late 1989. At that point, women's periodicals published between 1972 and 1985 will become immensely more accessible (Rooney, 1987).

Newly discovered information on women should be incorporated as soon as possible not only into women's studies courses, but into what is taught in all pertinent courses at university. This integration is rare and sporadic at Canadian universities, but has been systematically carried out on some American campuses. In the early 1980s, there were 49 integrationist projects underway in the United States (Bowles and Klein, 1983, p. 3). (Some of the national American bodies that financed women's educational institutions and projects in the 1970s no longer do so. The National Science Foundation has abolished its women's program and

National Environment and Health now does little. Emboldened by these cutbacks, conservative movements at the state level are also lobbying against women's studies programs for reasons such as that they promote lesbianism [Stimpson, 1984].)

The American Fund for the Improvement of Post-Secondary Education (FIPSE) has financed a number of large projects aimed at increasing the content and perspective on women in American higher education. Wheaton College, a small liberal arts and science institution for women in Massachusetts which received one of these grants, began in 1980 a three-year project whose aim was to incorporate the new scholarship on women into the curriculum at the level of introductory courses. In 1983, 250 women and men attended a conference held at Wheaton to discuss how it and other universities and colleges have gone about increasing course content on women, and how successful their efforts have been. The proceedings are published as *Toward a Balanced Curriculum: A Sourcebook for Initiating Gender Integration Projects* (1984), edited by Bonnie Spanier, Alexander Bloom, and Darlene Boroviak. This book includes examples of how teachers in a variety of disciplines reorganized their course material and method of instruction, and an extensive bibliography of books and articles on the same topic.

The project at Wheaton College was implemented in stages:

- Involving the faculty. The President and Provost, both women, strongly supported the project and, after considerable wide-ranging debate, the faculty as a whole agreed to apply for a FIPSE grant. Eventually over half the faculty became involved "in integration activities aimed at revising the curriculum to reflect women's experiences as well as those of men"; no faculty members had to become involved against their will.

- Generating specific proposals. Workshops were held during each January break to introduce faculty to ongoing work on women in the various disciplines. From these, individual faculty members and departments mapped out how specific courses would be reorganized. Teachers needed extra time and often money to prepare this new course material.

- Implementing changes. These changes were different for every discipline and depended on the attitude of the faculty and students involved, and the nature of the discipline. Innovation and enthusiasm were probably the two main keys to success.

- Assessment of changes. Statistics can be gathered on how much more about women has been incorporated into the syllabi, how many more books by women are being bought and read, and how many more papers dealing with women are being written by students and faculty. Anecdotal evidence will show whether more students and faculty are interested in, and learning about, women.

- Institutionalizing the changes. It is relatively easy to implement change, but difficult to ensure that it will not be downgraded in time, once faculty members who are enthusiastic feminists have left or retired and the freshness of the new ideas fades. Whether Wheaton College will continue to pursue a balanced curriculum in the future remains to be seen. (Spanier, Bloom, and Boroviak, 1984).

So far we have discussed the need to modify course material so that women and women's concerns are given adequate consideration. Since the "accepted" body of knowledge is conservative in every discipline, making change difficult even if money is available to facilitate it, universities should encourage students to work independent of regular courses. Women and men would learn a great deal if they were frequently allowed to go to original primary sources to gather material from which they could make generalizations and write papers. In addition, it would help to hold workshops in which feminist ideas and teaching were discussed with women faculty in *every* discipline (Bunch and Powell, 1983, p. 314).

Research (Chapter 6)

If we are to unearth more knowledge about women, we need more research which is both about women and from women's perspective. We need far less money spent on masculine interests (such as armaments) and far more on feminine concerns (such as natural reproduction and social and economic equality for women). The Social Sciences and Humanities Research Council of Canada should fund more research on women, preferably not only on set themes, such as the Women and Work Strategic Grant Program, but on what women want and need to know about. There should be more feminists on the juries that decide what projects should be supported, and more feminist journals funded so that women have more chance to publish their work. Mainstream academic journals should also be encouraged, perhaps by subsidies, to publish woman-centred articles on women and women's concerns.

Most important, research on women should be viewed as a serious and valid undertaking, and should be as likely to win a professor tenure as is doing research on any other topic. *Doing Feminist Research* (1981), edited by Helen Roberts, gives good examples of research carried out by feminists in the social sciences, as does *Taking Sex into Account* (1984), edited by Jill McCalla Vickers.

One group of feminists believes that all research in women's studies should have practical application, so that there is constant interaction between non-academic women and their privileged academic sisters. Maria Mies, for example, proposes the following postulates:

- The feminist researcher must openly state her biases, or conscious partiality, which goes beyond mere subjectivity.
- The researcher must view her material from below, rather than from above as is usual.
- She must actively participate in the women's liberation movement so that she is not an uninvolved spectator lacking inside knowledge.
- The research must be based on a commitment to change the status quo.
- The research must be pursued in order to act.
- Women's individual and social histories must be studied so that women can make plans for women's future based on their past.
- Women must discuss their experience and generalize from it in order to understand how society deprives individual women. (Bowles and Klein, 1983, p. 19)

Other feminists would undoubtedly add that:

- Social sciences should be concerned with more qualitative and less quantitative research, because the latter can be more readily used to control people rather than learn about them.
- Statistical surveys and participant observations in social science investigation should be replaced with experiential analysis, which takes both the experiences of the researcher and of the researched into account.
- Research should not centre on proving that which enhances the status quo, but should focus instead on clarifying those important matters that are unclear and ambiguous.

It is important that more feminists become administrators, so that far-reaching decisions take into consideration women's experiences and perspectives.

More women professors should also be hired, so that the proportion of women on faculties is similar to the proportion of women among academics who have earned their doctorates. In time, we hope that every discipline will have as many female as male professors.

One way to encourage universities to hire more women faculty (which they are now unwilling to do) is to provide government grants for this specific purpose as the Secretary of State has done in its Chairs in Women's Studies Program. Alternately, universities could lose funding if they continue to discriminate against female applicants. At York University, President Harry Arthurs developed a strategy to deal with the problem of departments not hiring many women. Previously, only one in four successful applicants being hired was a woman. Arthurs told department heads that if they exceeded their previous record of hiring women, they would receive a department bonus. In 1986, 40 per cent of faculty hired at York were women (*Globe and Mail,* March 4, 1987). There had been no quotas set, no backlash against quotas, the hiring was voluntary, and more women are now professors.

Once women are hired as professors, they should have the same chance as men to do research, to win tenure, and to earn salary increases. Most, if not all Canadian universities, pay women less well than men, so there must be constant vigilance to prevent this systemic discrimination. Jeremiah Allen (1984) has published a manual to indicate how such discrimination can be detected and thus addressed.

There will always need to be part-time teachers at universities, given the flexible nature of timetabling and student enrolments, and these jobs should have more status than at present, with benefits, research possibilities, and pay comparable to that received for similar teaching by full-time professors.

Both full-time and part-time women teachers would probably like to take advantage of sponsorship programs arranged by each university whereby a more experienced professor would work with a newly appointed one to ease her into her department. Such a relationship might also be academic, with the two professors collaborating on research.

In November, 1986, the Canadian Association of University Teachers published in the CAUT *Bulletin* an extensive plan called "Employment Equity for Women Academics: A Positive Action Strategy," which was devised by the Ontario Confederation of University Faculty Associations. It deals in depth with Pre-recruitment: Enlarging the pool of women candidates; Recruitment of candidates; Hiring; and Tenure and promotion. In the same issue, the CAUT has an extensive Policy Statement on Positive Action to Improve the Status of Women in Canadian Universities (pp. 22ff).

The most poorly paid employees at universities are women staff. These people have relatively little trouble being hired, because few men will compete for such lowly positions, but the work is monotonous, has little status, and often less dignity — as when a secretary, whatever her age, is referred to as "my girl." We would like to see universities lead society in its treatment of staff, as befits rational and intellectual institutions (see Council of Ontario Universities *Committee News*, May, 1987). Workers should help create their own environment and timetables rather than be treated like children.

University Services (Chapter 8)

Reasonably sized women's centres should be present at all universities so that women students have a safe place where they receive support and services. These centres should be well funded so that they need not spend large amounts of time scrambling for money; the value of such centres would more than warrant almost any amount of financial support.

In its November, 1986, *Bulletin*, the CAUT has an article entitled "Care of children is an equity issue." Inadequate childcare facilities virtually cripple many women students, researchers, and faculty, yet in 1984–85 there were only about .005 childcare spaces for each full-time university student or teacher (p. 21). All universities should have enough childcare facilities so that any parents who wish to make use of them may do so. Childcare should be available on a short-term or long-term basis, in the daytime and in the evening, and for children of all ages. If parents cannot afford the fees, these should be subsidized.

Universities should make provision for the realities of the lives of students who have children in their care. This needs to include such considerations as allowing them to rewrite a test missed because of a child's sickness, allowing extra time for the completion of essays and projects, making part-time studies a practical alternative through better funding , and instituting a leave-of-absence policy which does not jeopardize a student's standing in a program.

Because physical activity is important for health, and because sports are subsidized from university funding and student fees, they should be as readily available to women as to men. There should be as many sports — and as much money — available for women as men, and previously unathletic women especially should be encouraged to participate, to make up for society's perception of sports as a male domain. The University of Calgary, and some other universities, have set up mixed-sex teams that have a set minimum number of women players; this is a good way to interest women in a variety of sports. Since women are interested in aerobics, fitness, and aquatics, these activities should be provided at times throughout the day. Sports such as football and hockey cost a great deal of money. Money spent on these sports which comes out of university funds should be matched by money spent on women's sports.

The Women's Representative Committee of the Canadian Inter-university Athletic Union works to improve the status of women in university athletics. In early 1987, it sponsored a National Leadership Conference on Women in University Sport at Concordia University to which 100 female sport administrators and student leaders were invited. Its purpose was to facilitate change for and by present and future women administrators in university sport. It is also planning teaching sessions for women coaches in volleyball and basketball.

Universities should be sensitive to services that benefit women and men differently. Drug plans that do not cover birth control pills, reception rooms that welcome men but are inhospitable to women, and outdoor lighting systems that are suitable for men but leave women open to assault should be reconsidered carefully. All universities should have birth control centres where free counselling and advice are available.

Sexism, Sexual Harassment, and Violence (Chapter 9)

Universities should refuse to allow sexist messages or pictures on their property or in their literature, any more than they would condone racism. If students are caught defacing furniture, they should be charged with vandalizing, which is what they are doing. Library carrels which are covered with anti-women messages (as at Trent University) should be scrubbed frequently (as are desks at the University of Waterloo). Universities that collect stu-

123

dent money for extra-curricular activities should no longer do this for student newspapers that carry sexist content or groups that sponsor sexist events. If the administration makes it clear that sexism is unacceptable at a university, then professors and students will have at least to appear to follow its lead.

The problem of sexist professors can be addressed at workshops in which experienced leaders explain why women are offended by some professors' behavior, and in reports or columns in newsletters that are read by faculty. Often a teacher is unaware that his manner, or jokes, or course content annoy women and make it hard for them to learn. If professors persist in using sexist behavior, they should be denied merit pay, since their teaching is biased, insensitive, and therefore inadequate. A question concerning professors' sexist bias should be added to students' course evaluation forms.

It is difficult to know how to deal with the many people at universities who are openly anti-feminist. Professors can insist on the use of non-sexist language in essays and in the classroom (see Katz, 1981; Rancy and Sah, 1984), but their insistence may raise a backlash against feminists. Anti-women sentiments will only really be addressed when they are seen by everyone to be as abhorrent as racist sentiments.

Sexual harassment has existed for centuries, but it has only been a decade since it has been recognized as a serious social issue; before that it was considered a part of "normal" male behavior (Hornosty, 1986). Probably York University has addressed sexual harassment as seriously as any campus, although now 18 universities have policies or procedures in place to deal with it. The Canadian Association of University Teachers has a policy statement on it, and its Board has approved a Model Clause on Sexual Harassment (CAUT, July, 1987; CAUT *Bulletin,* November, 1986, p. 19).

The two-room office of York University's Sexual Harassment Education and Complaint Centre is staffed by two part-time co-ordinators. It serves the surrounding area, not just the university, and had about 35 complaints in the 1986–87 year (Gill Teiman, personal communication, April 28, 1987), a small fraction of the incidents that occur. Each complaint is dealt with only to the extent that the victim wishes. The co-ordinator arranges for someone to talk to the harasser, if this is appropriate, and tries to effect an informal solution. This formal procedure is time-consuming and rarely used, since social attitudes in general and the extensive unionization at York in particular almost guarantee that the victim will lose. The co-ordinators talk to groups and publicize the centre whenever possible to alert people to the seriousness of sexual harassment. The extensive *Report of the Presidential Advisory Committee on Sexual Harassment* (York University, 1982), which is soon to be updated, includes a large bibliography. Another useful resource is *Against Sexual Harassment: A Handbook for Students at Post-Secondary Educational Institutions in British Columbia* (1985) put out by the British Columbia Public Interest Research Group.

Appropriate action should be taken to combat sexual assaults. Lighting on campuses should be bright, especially around parking lots, and security offices should provide information on the numbers and locations of attacks on campus. Carleton University's Women's Centre has a campus map displayed on which women can mark areas which they know or feel are unsafe. Some universities have escort services and safety vans that women can use at night to go from one area of campus to another or to leave the university. At York University in February 1987, for example, 955 men and 2916 women used the Student Escort Service (*Excalibur,* April 9, 1987). However, beneficial though this service is, the fact that children are not allowed to ride in the vans severely limits its usefulness to women — the very people whose safety it is intended to foster (personal communication, December 19, 1987).

There is controversy about the use of security officers, especially if these have not been well trained. Many people would like their number to be increased, so that their presence will deter crime. Others find the existence of security officers problematic (*Excalibur,* April 9, 1987). Such officers, who are usually men, may eventually be able to use handcuffs, billy clubs, tear gas, and guns to enforce their powers; like some police, those men and their weapons may not be sympathetic to women. Police have a poor record in dealing with rape and domestic violence which does not make many women optimistic about more security officers being a solution to possible violence. Universities might better work toward creating safe environments on their campuses.

* * *

We hope that this book will both enlighten readers about how their tax dollars are being spent at Canadian universities, and provoke discussion about what can be done concerning present inequities. Any number of recommendations about women can be suggested to universities, but they will be of little avail if a climate of goodwill toward women is not present; administrators and professors can always dream up reasons why specific actions that would benefit women should not be taken. They may fear change, or they may actually believe that women do not belong equally with men at our universities. We ask these people to be rational, not emotional. We want them to understand that women have as much right as men to education and scholarship. Canada needs to make use of all the talents its citizens possess. This can only come about if as many women as men teach at universities, and if what they teach has as much a feminist as a male bias.

Selected Bibliography

Ad Hoc Committee on the Status of Women. 1986, January. *A Future for Women at the University of Toronto.* Toronto: University of Toronto.

Alcock, John. 1984. *Animal Behavior: An Evolutionary Approach.* Sunderland, MA: Sinauer Associates.

Allen, Jeremiah. 1984. *Manual for Determination of Academic Salary Discrimination against Women.* Ottawa: Canadian Association of University Teachers.

Altman, Leslie. 1980. Christine de Pisan: First professional woman of letters (1364–1430?). In J. R. Brink, Ed., *Female Scholars: A Tradition of Learning before 1800,* pp. 7–23. Montreal: Eden Press.

Anon. 1987, January. A personal perspective. *Stamp Out Sexism: The Newsletter of the Coalition for Voices against Sexism,* 1: 4–6. (Available from Women's Centre, Queen's University, Kingston).

Association of Universities and Colleges of Canada. 1985. *Academic and Administrative Officers at Canadian Universities 1985–86.* Ottawa: AUCC.

Bart, Pauline. 1987, February. Rape avoidance. *The Second Decade Status of Women Newsletter,* pp. 1–2. Downsview, Ont: York University.

Baxter, Bryane. 1987. *The University of Toronto Women's Centre.* Toronto: Women's Centre, University of Toronto.

Bercuson, David J., Robert Bothwell, and J. L. Granatstein. 1984. *The Great Brain Robbery.* Toronto: McClelland and Stewart.

Bezucha, Robert J. 1985. Feminist pedagogy as a subversive activity. In Margo Culley, and Catherine Portuges, Eds., *Gendered Subjects,* pp. 81–95. Boston: Routledge and Kegan Paul.

Black, Naomi. 1987, February. Editorial *The Second Decade status of Women Newsletter,* p. 2. Downsview, Ont: York University.

_____. 1988, January. Ontario's Faculty Renewal Fund and the Status of women — 'little now remains besides some pious hopes . . .'' Letter to the editor. *University Affairs,* 29, 1: 16.

Bowles, Gloria, and Renate Duelli Klein, Eds. 1983. *Theories of Women's Studies.* London and New York: Routledge and Kegan Paul.

Branscombe, Lewis M. 1979. Women in science. *Science,* 205, 4408 : 751.

Bristol Women's Studies Group. 1979. *Half the Sky. An Introduction to Women's Studies.* London: Virago.

Brodribb, Somer. 1983, November. Women studies Canada 1983; Canadian universities: a learning environment for women? *Resources for Feminist Research,* 12, 3: 53–71.

_____. 1987. Women's Studies in Canada. *Resources for Feminist Research,* Special Publication.

Bunch, Charlotte, and Betty Powell. 1983. Charlotte Bunch and Betty Powell talk about feminism, Blacks, and education as politics. In Charlotte Bunch, and Sandra Pollack, Eds., *Learning Our Way: Essays in Feminist Education*, pp. 302–316. Trumansburg, NY: Crossing Press.

Burger, Anne. 1986, December. *Report on Sexual Harassment and Sexual Assault at Simon Fraser University.* Vancouver: British Columbia Public Interest Research Group.

Canadian Association of University Teachers. 1986a. *Brief to the Special Committee on Child Care.* Ottawa: CAUT.

————. 1986b. *Employee Benefits Survey for Faculty in the Atlantic Provinces; Employee Benefits Survey for Faculty in the Western Provinces.* Ottawa: CAUT.

————. 1986c. *Library Salary Survey 1984–85.* Ottawa: CAUT.

————. 1987. *Sexual Harassment Policies (18 Canadian universities plus 3 national model policies).* Ottawa: CAUT.

Canadian Federation of Students. 1986. *Student Association Directory, 1986–87.* Ottawa: CFS.

Canadian Interuniversity Athletic Union 1982.. *A Comparative Study: Relative opportunities for women in the CIAU.* Update 1981–82. Ottawa: CIAU.

————. 1983, June. *Report of the CIAU Women's Representative Committee.* Ottawa: CIAU.

————. 1986, June. Women's Representative Committee report, *Proceedings of the Ninth General Assembly Meeting,* Appendix G, 1–3. Ottawa: CIAU.

————. 1987. *A Comparative Study: Relative opportunities for women in the CIAU.* Draft Version. Ottawa: CIAU.

Chalmers, John W., Ed. 1979. *The Alberta Diamond Jubilee Anthology.* Edmonton: Hurtig.

Chimming, Sharon, with Julie George. 1986. *Confronting Sexual Harassment on Campus.* Waterloo: Federation of Students, University of Waterloo.

Collins, Trudi. 1986, November 25. Engineering from the inside. *Otherwise,* University of Toronto.

Commonwealth Universities Yearbook. 1985. London: Association of Commonwealth Universities.

Cude, Wilfred. 1987. *The PhD Trap.* West Bay, N.S.: Medicine Label Press.

Culley, Margo, and Johnnella E. Butler. 1984. Black studies and women's studies: An overdue partnership. In Bonnie Spanier, Alexander Bloom, and Darlene Boroviak, Eds., *Toward a Balanced Curriculum,* pp. 109–116. Cambridge, MA: Schenkman Publishing.

————, and Catherine Portuges, Eds. 1985. *Gendered Subjects: The Dynamics of Feminist Teaching.* Boston: Routledge and Kegan Paul.

Dagg, Anne Innis. 1983. *Harems and Other Horrors: Sexual Bias in Behavioral Biology.* Waterloo, Ont: Otter Press.

_____. 1984, March-April. Sexual bias in the literature of social behaviour in mammals and birds. *International Journal of Women's Studies,* 7, 2: 118-135.

_____. 1984b. January-February. Sexism in the University of Waterloo Calendar. *Language Alert Newsletter,* 4: 4-5. Available from Box 747, Waterloo, Ont, N2J 4C2.

_____. 1985, Fall. The status of some Canadian women PhD scientists. *Atlantis,* 11,1: 66–77.

_____. 1987. *Manipulation of Statistics to Suppress Information.* Manuscript submitted for publication.

_____. 1986. *The Fifty Per Cent Solution: Why Should Women Pay for Men's Culture?* Waterloo, Ont: Otter Press.

_____. 1988. *The Absence of Topics of Special Interest to Women in General Psychology Textbooks.* Manuscript submitted for publication.

Ehrenreich, Barbara, and Dierdre English. 1979. *For Her Own Good. 150 Years of the Experts' Advice to Women.* Garden City, NY: Anchor Press.

Eichler, Margrit. 1985. And the work never ends: feminist contributions. *Canadian Review of Sociology and Anthropology,* 22: 619-644.

_____, and Jeanne Lapointe. 1985. *On the Treatment of the Sexes in Research.* Ottawa: Social Sciences and Humanities Research Council of Canada.

Finn, Geraldine. 1982. On the oppression of women in philosophy — or, whatever happened to objectivity? In Angela Miles, and Geraldine Finn, Eds., *Feminism in Canada: From Pressure to Politics,* pp. 145–173. Montreal: Black Rose Books.

FitzGerald, Maureen, Connie Guberman, and Margie Wolfe, Eds. 1982. *Still Ain't Satisfied!* Toronto: Women's Press.

Ford, Anne Rochon. 1985. *A Path Not Strewn with Roses: One Hundred Years of Women at the University of Toronto 1884–1984.* Toronto: University of Toronto Press.

Franklin, Phyllis, et al. 1981. *Sexual and Gender Harassment in the Academy. A Guide for Faculty, Students, and Administrators.* New York: Modern Language Association of America.

Franklin, Ursula Martius, et al. 1984. *Knowledge Reconsidered: A Feminist Overview.* Ottawa: Canadian Research Institute for the Advancement of Women.

Franzosa, Susan Douglas, and Karen A. Mazza. 1984. *Integrating Women's Studies in the Curriculum. An Annotated Bibliography.* Westport, CT: Greenwood Press.

Gilbert, Sandra M., and Susan Gubar. 1985. *The Norton Anthology of Literature by Women: The Tradition in English.* 4th Edition. New York: Norton.

Grassick, Patrick. 1987, February. U. of Calgary appeals court decision in hiring case of Prof. Vinogradov. CAUT *Bulletin,* p. 9.

Graves, Joan. 1986. *Discrimination on the basis of sex? Not at UVic?!* Vancouver: BC Public Interest Research Group.

Greenglass, Esther R. 1982. *A World of Difference. Gender Roles in Perspective.* Toronto: Wiley.

Groark, Leo. 1983, Fall. Beyond affirmative action. *Atlantis,* 9, 1: 13-24.

Haley, Ella. 1985. Exploratory Study of Factors Affecting Graduate Students' Performance. Unpublished master's thesis, Department of Sociology, University of Waterloo.

Hall, M. Ann, and Dorothy A. Richardson. 1982. *Fair Ball: Towards Sex Equality in Canadian Sport.* Ottawa: Canadian Advisory Council on the Status of Women.

Hall, Roberta, M., and Bernice R. Sandler. 1982. *The Classroom Climate: A Chilly One for Women?* Washington, D.C.: Project on the Status and Education of Women, Association of American Colleges.

Harper, J. Russell. 1977. *Painting in Canada: A History.* Toronto: University of Toronto Press.

Harris, Robin S. 1976. *A History of Higher Education in Canada 1863–1960.* Toronto: University of Toronto Press.

Harrison, Deborah. 1987, June. The story of Brock secretary Mary Warner. CAUT *Bulletin,* p. 9.

Haskins, Charles Homer. 1984. *The Rise of Universities.* Ithaca, NY: Cornell University Press.

Holleran, Paula R. 1985. The feminist curriculum: Issues for survival in academe. *Journal of Thought,* 20: 25–36.

Hornosty, Jennie. 1986, November. Sexual harassment: It's everyone's business. CAUT *Bulletin,* p. 19.

Howe, Florence. 1984. *Myths of Coeducation. Selected Essays, 1964–1983.* Bloomington: Indiana University Press.

Howell, Sandi, and Irene Harris. 1987, December. Bargaining and lobbying for pay equity. *Breaking the Silence,* 6, 2: 13–15.

Hunter College Women's Studies Collective. 1983. *Women's Realities, Women's Choices. An Introduction to Women's Studies.* New York: Oxford University Press.

Iacobucci, Frank. 1984, June. Report of the Department of Architecture Review Committee. Toronto: University of Toronto.

Kahan, Marcia. 1985, April. Pillow talk. *Books in Canada,* pp. 3–4.

Kantaroff, Maryon. 1975. Celebrating the egg. *Emergency Librarian,* 2, 4/5: 6–14.

Katz, Wendy R. 1981. *Her and His: Language of Equal Value.* Halifax: Status of Women, Nova Scotia Confederation of University Faculty Associations.

Kealey, Linda, Ed. 1979. *A Not Unreasonable Claim: Women and Reform in Canada 1880s–1920s.* Toronto: Women's Press.

Kramarae, Cheris, and Paula A. Treichler. 1987. *A Feminist Dictionary.* Boston: Pandora.

Kymlicka, Will. 1987, February 6. Feminists want better forum for discussion, not monopoly. Letter to the editor. *Queen's Journal.*

Leach, Belinda, Ellen Lesiuk, and Penny E. Morton. 1986, Spring. Perceptions of fear in the urban environment. *Women and Environments,* 9, 2: 10–12.

Leonard, Elizabeth Lindeman. 1986, Summer. Faculty women for equity: a class-action suit against the state of Oregon. *Affilia,* pp. 6–19.

Longford, Elizabeth. 1986. *The Pebbled Shore: The Memoirs of Elizabeth Longford.* London: Weidenfeld and Nicolson.

Losel-Wieland-Engelmann, Berta. 1981, Fall. Feminist repercussions of a literary research project. *Atlantis,* 6, 1: 84-90.

Mazur, Carol, and Sheila Pepper, Compilers. 1984. *Women in Canada. A Bibliography 1965 to 1982.* Toronto: OISE Press.

McDaniel, Susan. 1987, March. Just Gender. *University of Waterloo Courier,* pp. 2–6.

McInnes-Hayman, Sasha. 1980. *Contemporary Canadian Women Artists: A Survey.* Ottawa: Status of Women Canada. [Note: McInnes-Hayman has, since these publications appeared, returned to her birth name, Sasha McInnes. It is in this name that her more recent writings and art works are available.]

——————. 1981, July. *Representation of Female and Male Artists in Canadian Art History Texts Used in the Visual Art Department, University of Western Ontario, 1980–1981.* London, Ont: University of Western Ontario. [See note above.]

McIntyre, Sheila. 1987, January. Gender bias within a Canadian Law School. CAUT *Bulletin,* pp. 7–11.

Megaw, W. J. 1986, September. Girls' physics workshops at York. *Physics in Canada,* p. 108.

Miles, Angela, and Geraldine Finn. 1982. *Feminism in Canada: From Pressure to Politics.* Montreal: Black Rose Books.

Miller, Casey, and Kate Swift. 1977. *Words and Women: New Language in New Times.* Garden City, NY: Anchor/Doubleday.

Neatby, Hilda. 1978. *Queen's University. Vol. 1: 1841–1917: To Strive, To Seek, To Find, And Not To Yield.* Montreal: McGill-Queen's University Press.

Nelson, Sharon. 1982. Bemused, branded, and belittled. Women and writing in Canada. *Fireweed,* 15: 65–102.

O'Brien, Mary. 1981. *The Politics of Reproduction.* Boston: Routledge and Kegan Paul.

Ontario Ministry of Education and Ministry of Colleges and Universities. 1987. *Employment survey of 1985 graduates of Ontario universities.* Toronto: Ontario Ministry of Education and Ministry of Colleges and Universities.

Ontario Task Force on Equal Opportunity in Athletics. 1984. *Can I Play?* Vol. 2. Toronto: Ontario Ministry of Labour.

Pierson, Ruth, and Alison Prentice. 1982. Feminism and the writing and teaching of history. In Angela Miles, and Geraldine Finn, Eds., *Feminism in Canada: From Pressure to Politics,* pp. 103-118. Montreal: Black Rose Books.

Pitt, D. G. 1984. *E. J. Pratt: The Truant Years, 1882-1927.* Toronto: University of Toronto Press.

Pomfret, Marilyn. 1986. Toward equivalence of opportunity. In A. W.

Taylor, Ed., *The Role of Interuniversity Athletics: A Canadian Perspective*, pp. 83-88. London, Ont: Sports Dynamics.

Powe, Bruce. 1981. The university as the hidden ground of Canadian literature. *Antigonish Review*, 47: 11–15.

Professional Women's Association. 1986. *A Study on Part-Time Academic Faculty and Staff.* Waterloo: University of Waterloo.

Rancy, Catherine, and Manju Sah. 1984. *Guidelines for Non-Sexist Writing.* Ottawa: Canadian Advisory Council on the Status of Women.

Reid, Dennis. 1973. *A Concise History of Canadian Painting.* Toronto: Oxford University Press.

Rich, Adrienne. 1979. *On Lies, Secrets, and Silence.* New York: Norton.

Roberts, Helen, Ed. 1981. *Doing Feminist Research.* London: Routledge and Kegan Paul.

Rooney, Frances. 1987, November. Some feminist resources. *Ethics in Education,* 7, 2: 16.

Rosenburg, Rosalind. 1982. *Beyond Separate Spheres.* New Haven: Yale University Press.

Ross, Alexander. 1974. *The College on the Hill. A History of the Ontario Agricultural College, 1874–1974.* Toronto: Copp Clark.

Ryten, E. December 1986/January 1987. Undergraduate enrolment in Canadian faculties of medicine. *Association of Canadian Medical Colleges Forum,* 20, 1: 8–10.

Schmitz, Betty. 1985. *Integrating Women's Studies into the Curriculum: A Guide and Bibliography.* Old Westbury, New York: Feminist Press.

Simeone, Angela. 1987. *Academic Women: Working Towards Equality.* South Hadley, MA: Bergin and Garvey.

Social Sciences and Humanities Research Council of Canada. 1986. *Annual Report, 1985–86.* Ottawa: SSHRCC.

Spanier, Bonnie, Alexander Bloom, and Darlene Boroviak, Eds. 1984. *Toward a Balanced Curriculum: A Sourcebook for Initiating Gender Integration Projects.* Cambridge, MA: Schenkman Publishing.

Spender, Dale. 1981. *Men's Studies Modified: The Impact of Feminism on the Academic Disciplines.* Oxford: Pergamon Press.

_____. 1982. *Invisible Women: The Schooling Scandal.* London: Writers and Readers.

Statistics Canada. 1971. *Survey of Higher Education, Part 1: Fall Enrolment in Universities and Colleges, 1969–70.* Catalogue No. 81-204. Ottawa: Ministry of Supply and Services.

_____. 1977. *Universities: Enrolment and Degrees, 1975–76.* Catalogue No. 81-204. Ottawa: Ministry of Supply and Services.

_____. 1986a. *Universities: Enrolment and Degrees, 1984.* Catalogue No. 81-204. Ottawa: Ministry of Supply and Services.

_____. 1986b. *Teachers in Universities, 1984–85.* Catalogue No. 81-241. Ottawa: Ministry of Supplies and Services.

Stimpson, Catharine. 1984. Where does integration fit: the development of women's studies. In Bonnie Spanier, Alexander Bloom, and Darlene Boroviak, Eds., *Toward a Balanced Curriculum,* pp. 11-24. Cambridge, MA: Schenkman Publishing.

Stineman, Esther. 1979. *Women's Studies. A Recommended Core Bibliography*. Littleton, CO: Libraries Unlimited.

Strong-Boag, Veronica, and Anita Clair Fellman, Eds. 1986. *Rethinking Canada. The Promise of Women's History*. Toronto: Copp Clark Pitman.

Support Group. 1985. *Murmurs of the Heart: Issues for women in medical training*. Toronto: Faculty of Medicine, University of Toronto.

Symons, T. H., and J. E. Page. 1984. *Some Questions of Balance: Human Resources, Higher Education and Canadian Studies*. Ottawa: Association of Universities and Colleges of Canada.

Thibault, Gisele Marie. 1987. *The Dissenting Feminist Academy: A History of the Barriers to Feminist Scholarship*. New York: Peter Lang.

Thompson, Jane L. 1983. *Learning Liberation. Women's Response to Men's Education*. London: Croom Helm.

Tiffany, Sharon W., Ed. 1979. *Women and Society. An Anthropological Reader*. Montreal: Eden Press.

Toogood, D. J. 1987, January 30. Recruitment of feminists curbs academic freedom. Letter to the editor. *Queen's Journal*.

Turner, Joan, and Lois Emery, Eds. 1983. *Perspectives on Women in the 1980s*. Winnipeg: University of Manitoba Press.

Van Kirk, Sylvia. 1983. *Many Tender Ties: Women in Fur-Trade Society: 1670–1870*. Norman, OK: University of Oklahoma Press.

Vickers, Jill McCalla, Ed. 1984. *Taking Sex into Account: The Policy Consequences of Sexist Research*. Ottawa: Carleton University Press.

————— , and June Adam. 1977. *But Can You Type? Canadian Universities and the Status of Women*. Ottawa: Canadian Association of University Teachers.

Waite, Peter. 1987. Between three oceans: challenges of a continental destiny 1840–1900. In Craig Brown, Ed., *The Illustrated History of Canada*, pp. 279–374. Toronto: Lester and Orpen Dennys.

Williams, Andrea. 1987, March 12. Sexist propaganda and the 'sacred Vic muff.' *The Varsity*, University of Toronto.

Wilson, Edward O. 1975. *Sociobiology: The New Synthesis*. Cambridge, MA: Belknap Press.

Wilson, S. J. 1982. *Women, the Family, and the Economy*. Toronto: McGraw-Hill Ryerson.

Wine, Jeri Dawn. 1982. Gynocentric values and feminist psychology. In Angela Miles, and Geraldine Finn, Eds., *Feminism in Canada: From Pressue to Politics*, pp. 67–87. Montreal: Black Rose Books.

Yates, J. Michael, Ed. 1970. *Contemporary Poetry of British Columbia*. Vancouver: Sono Nis Press.

Zerker, Sally. 1987, March. *The Innis Years at the University of Toronto: 1920-1952*. Paper presented at the Harold Innis Conference/Workshop, Toronto, Ont.

We have consulted the following university newspapers:

Charlatan	Carleton University
The Cord	Sir Wilfrid Laurier University
The Energizer	University of Toronto
Excalibur	York University
The Gargoyle	University College, University of Toronto
The Gazette	University of Waterloo
Imprint	University of Waterloo
Innis Herald	Innis College, University of Toronto
Iron Warrier	University of Waterloo
The Lexicon	York University
The New Edition	University of Toronto
The Newspaper	University of Toronto
Ontarion	University of Guelph
Otherwise	University of Toronto
The Peak	Simon Fraser University
Queen's Journal	Queen's University
The Strand	University of Toronto
Toike	University of Toronto
Ubyssey	University of British Columbia
The Varsity	University of Toronto

"How's your daughter?"

"Oh, she's fine. I told her she could live at home if she wanted to go to graduate school, but she'd have to pay her own expenses. So she comes here to classes, goes to work, then comes back here to study. She leaves when the library closes, gets home at 1:30 or 2:00 a.m. She asked me to lend her $3000 to buy a car. She's only had the job a month. I told her no way would a bank lend her the money and no way would I lend it to her. You know what she said? She said, 'It takes me an hour and a half to get home at night and I have to walk across a dark campus at midnight. You want me to get raped?' "

Both men laugh. "What did you say?"

"I said, 'I guess so.'"

"Your son still in graduate school?"

"Yeah. He costs enough without putting money into her, too."

Two faculty members,
Ontario university campus, 1986